WHEN REALITY BITES

WHEN REALITY BITES

How Denial Helps and What to Do When It Hurts

HOLLY PARKER, PhD

Hazelden Publishing

Hazelden Publishing
Center City, Minnesota 55012
hazelden.org/bookstore

Library of Congress Cataloging-in-Publication Data

Names: Parker, Holly (Psychologist), author.
Title: When reality bites : how denial helps and what to do when it hurts / Holly Parker.
Description: Center City, MN : Hazelden, 2016.
Identifiers: LCCN 2016018401 (print) | LCCN 2016029872 (ebook) | ISBN 9781616496654 (paperback) | ISBN 9781616496975 (e-book)
Subjects: LCSH: Denial (Psychology) | Defense mechanisms (Psychology) | Self-deception.
Classification: LCC BF175.5.D44 .P37 2016 (print) | LCC BF175.5.D44 (ebook) | DDC 158.1--dc23
LC record available at https://urldefense.proofpoint.com/v2/url?u=https-3A__lccn.loc.gov_2016018401&d=CwIFAg&c=6ZBjJJ4GuzMgOe9TMyqXQw&r=0u0oQwzo-nFOsZfw7LTa_9nT8F0Eio9DTBOwNLsJNdk&m=BqI3nwGQJUJFrHJtNYL_7uHtxAwtwg4gDikUPm7cknI&s=lnnBUqoLnCon0Sw6GQhXpCQqluqwI_Qp9Fo5xC-mKmU&e=

Editor's note
The names, details, and circumstances may have been changed to protect the privacy of those mentioned in this publication.

This publication is not intended as a substitute for the advice of health care professionals.

Readers should be aware that websites listed in this work may have changed or disappeared between when this work was written and when it is read.

Alcoholics Anonymous, AA, and the Big Book are registered trademarks of Alcoholics Anonymous World Services, Inc.

20 19 18 17 16 1 2 3 4 5 6

Cover design: Terri Kinne
Interior design and typesetting: Percolator Graphic Design
Developmental editor: Sid Farrar
Production editor: Heather Silsbee

This book is dedicated to Guille, mi paraiso . . .

CONTENTS

ACKNOWLEDGMENTS

The experience of writing this book was meaningful, humbling, and wonderful, and I am indebted to the deeply good people who accompanied me along the way. Linda Konnor, my amazingly talented and kind agent—thank you so much for not only bringing the possibility of this project to my awareness, but for all of your support, attention, and guidance. I am lucky, to say the least. To my developmental editor, Sid Farrar, what an unbelievable privilege and joy it was to work with you. Your sage advice, superb editing, thoughtfulness, and encouragement throughout this process elevated the book and made me a better writer. I also want to heartily thank my production editor, Heather Silsbee, and my copyeditor, Betty Christiansen. Your edits and feedback were top-notch and exceedingly beneficial, for this book and for me. And of course, I'm extremely grateful to Hazelden Publishing. Thank you for believing in the importance of a book on denial, for trusting me to write it, and for pairing me with a stellar team. And ultimately, the whole point of this book is to go on a tour with you, Dear Reader, a tour that I know you could have chosen not to take. THANK YOU for your generous willingness to let me travel this journey with you, as you are where the meaningfulness of it all lies.

I also want to thank the mentors and students along the way who shared their insights, taught me, challenged me, and curiously explored with me, and who continue to do so. And to my greatest teachers, the courageous and exceptional individuals who have permitted me to walk alongside them in their own journeys of healing—I'm immensely grateful for the gift.

To my parents, thank you so much for all of your moral support throughout this process, and for sharing your wisdom and humor with me at all of the right times. To my parents-in-law, I am deeply thankful for a truly special friendship with you, and for all of your kindhearted support. My friends—a million thanks to you for your patience with me, and for being simply beautiful and inspiring. I also want to send barks and squawks of appreciation to my non-human friends, Edgar the Wild Man and Romeo the Wonder dog. We miss you, Romi. You live on in mirthful tales.

Most of all, I want to thank Guille, my husband, best friend, soulmate, and unquestionably better half. I don't have the words to tell you how much I treasure all that is you. Thank you for the unlimited love, encouragement, passion, coaching, patience, support, and hilarity you give me every day. This book would not be what it is without you, and this basement troll is forever in your debt.

INTRODUCTION

Life certainly is a radiant ride, with its generous helpings of love, joy, triumph, laughter, adventure, meaning, and all. Yet the joyride just as certainly intermixes worthy servings of wrangles, stumbling blocks, travails, and heartache along the way, doesn't it? It's unbelievable when you really stop and think about it. So how do we deal with the hardships and the awkwardness that come with being human?

Conveniently, we human folk have a real, ingrained knack for doing what, on its face, just seems like plain, time-honored good sense. We steer clear of what hurts. We dodge the unpleasant, the disquieting, and the monstrous. See the agreeable, convenient, and risk-free pussycat lying in the warm afternoon sun over there? We'd much rather cozy up to that sweet embodiment of domestication, and feel snug and invulnerable, than face the threatening tiger that the harshness of life can appear as at times. And this all-too-justifiable impulse to veer from the undesirable, whether we do so by pretending it doesn't exist or by dodging it, inhabits us all. There's no denying that we all deny. The tricky side of denial is that even though it allays our unease in the short run, over the long haul it can bite us in the rear end and take more away from us than it offers. Lamentably, this unjust exchange often transpires right under our noses and we miss it, leading us to continue wielding the same evasive tactics and getting nowhere or, in many cases, slumping downward.

At the same time, denial can be a first-class friend, giving us the hardiness we need to strive for what we cherish, to take risks and perform acts of heroism, to cope with threats, and to function and thrive day to day. The kernel of navigating denial is to boost the places where denial helps and shrink where it hinders, whenever possible.

Have you ever gone to a carnival or arcade? At many events like these, there is a game called Whac-a-Mole, which is played exactly as it sounds. There are a series of holes, and plastic moles pop up, one after the other. And what is your job? Your role is to bash each mole that pops up over the head with a hammer (albeit a soft one), before the mole descends back into the hole. This game is a pretty apt metaphor for denial, because denial doesn't just make its home within us. It pops up in a myriad of places, extending to our relationships, the society we dwell in, and the mega big picture of life and death, with its rewards and punishments at every level. Just like the toy moles that emerge, egging us on to take a whack, the doohickeys that distress us, embarrass us, and unsettle us spring up from life's sundry nooks, and it's utterly human to want to clobber them back down, filling the holes with concrete afterward.

In fact, to give you a sense of how life is just crawling with denial, let's stop for a moment and look at how, in a book on denial, I just used a game to illustrate denial, a game that probably requires denial to even work. As a society, we try to protect children from violence, and yet we skip over the obvious fact that at the core of this child's game is an essentially savage act. As you'll come to see as we walk through this book together, examples such as this are perplexing, yet understandable, and all too universal among humans. We are an enigmatic lot indeed!

This book explores the manifold spaces where denial pops up, swaying the course of personal wellness, intimate bonds, and social norms over a lifetime. It's about the imprints denial forms across your own life.

In the past, perhaps you've heard that denial is a defense mechanism that is always a sign of psychological dysfunction. That message is not happening here. Contrary to the idea that denial is pathological, this book presents denial as an expression of a perfectly rational desire to avoid pain, one that regrettably often winds up being fruitless or even harmful. Yet that's only one side of denial's face. The book also paints denial as a necessity that, on numerous occasions, is an extremely adaptive and healthy response. It gives us the comforts that we need to push through hard times, take risks, and function in daily life without panicking.

This book will take you on a guided tour of the ways we steer clear of unpleasant truths, giving it our all to seek contentment. Our voyage will be a somewhat paradoxical one, as we'll deal with denial head-on across six different levels of human life. We'll start from inside our bodies and minds, and move outward from there to our conscious thoughts and feelings, and then to our relationships with others and the situations we navigate. From there, we'll pan out to the social world we inhabit and beyond this to our life and death. We'll ponder the ways denial works for us, as well as the ways it reigns over us and bottles us up, keeping us from living the life we'd truly love. There will be plenty of stories and examples to showcase and illuminate what we learn. Throughout the book, at every stop, we'll pick up practicable solutions and guidance on how we can put an end to wielding denial in ways that work against us and step toward making denial work for us.

Just for the record, if you've ever beaten yourself up for being in denial, I really hope you'll stop. I know that's a cinch for me to say, and it may very well be pretty tough for you to do, but please try. Trust me, you're in good company—like, with everyone else on this planet. Denial and avoidance touch us all and often in countless ways. Through my clinical practice, the research I've read and conducted, and my experience as an ordinary human being in the world, I witness denial's profound and far-reaching capacity to both tear down and lift up.

Thankfully, we humans possess an awe-inspiring bravery that enables us to face denial, finding greater tranquility and liberation in the process. On the other hand, denial crucially spurs us on, lending us the pluck and fortitude that we need. As the popular saying goes, "denial ain't just a river in Egypt." True, and denial ain't always a bad thing, either.

This book is chock-full of the latest science on denial, and it also draws from my reflections and extensive clinical experience in this area. Although I designed the book to proceed in order through the various stops on the denial tour, you are welcome to focus on a particular stop sooner if it feels more pressing to you. This is a democratic book, so by all means, follow your gut and explore as you fancy.

If you're weighing whether this book is for you, good for you. Why spend your time on anything unless it really speaks to you, right? So let me clarify by telling you whom I had in mind when writing it. This book is for anyone who wishes to peek at the spaces where we hesitate to look. It speaks to people who seek a deeper, fuller understanding of how denial affects their lives, how they can recognize and break through denial, how it limits their options for living fully, and how they can hold on to the evasiveness of denial when it serves them well. I'm deeply passionate about this subject and believe in the radical changes that a healthy balance with denial brings, so I'm admittedly keeping my fingers (and toes) crossed that you'll take this tour with me. Regardless of what you decide, thank you kindly for taking the time to check out this book, and I wish you happiness, love, peacefulness, and a fabulous life.

1

IF DENIAL AIN'T JUST A RIVER, THEN WHAT IS IT?

The human mind isn't a terribly logical or consistent place. Most people, given the choice to face a hideous or terrifying truth or to conveniently avoid it, choose the convenience and peace of normality. That doesn't make them strong or weak people, or good or bad people. It just makes them people.

—Jim Butcher, *Turn Coat*

Guille, my delightful husband, took me out to dinner for my birthday. Now ordinarily, we opt for the pure and simple. Still, every now and then, we know how to revel in fine dining too. And for my birthday, Guille went all out. There we were, decked out in dashing duds in one of the most deluxe restaurants in Boston. Just a couple of tables away from us, Bill Belichick, head coach of the New England Patriots, chatted with his partner, whose sparkly dress bedazzled. A discreet legion of refined waitstaff breezed by to sleekly attend to our every need. You get the picture. Clearly, we had dropped anchor at ultra posh land. As we merrily noshed on the colorful, savory assortment of petit courses, I felt a tickle in my stomach. Well, actually, it was more like a twirl.

Huh, what's that? my brain gently inquired.

Right away, my mind chimed in. *Oh, it's nothing. You're just fine. It'll pass!*

Then, as the twirl in my body opted not to listen, it graduated to a spiral and a bit of nausea and sluggishness waltzed in to join the ball.

Intelligently piping in again, my brain cautioned, *Um, OK, this is weird. We're not feeling too dandy here. I think you might want to tell Guille.*

You would think that I'd listen to this sensible tip-off, considering that Guille is not only the love of my life, but also a physician. For all that, it didn't stop the clash of wills in my inner monologue from forging ahead as my mind gave a big thumbs-down to that idea.

Nah! Don't worry about it, my mind reassured. *Just sit back a little and try to tune it out. After all, what earthly reason could you have for feeling this way? None. It doesn't make any logical sense. I bet it's all in your head, so just relax and enjoy yourself, and this will all go away. You'll be fine!*

So I dutifully followed my mind's guidance, doing my utmost to brush it all off and swallow the notion that this was nothing more than hogwash. I followed it all the way until the wooziness finally bulldozed me into saying "uncle" and facing the naked truth that I was about to pass out. I hurriedly told Guille that I wasn't feeling up to par and swiftly excused myself to the restroom. I pretty near made it, but there was a sudden *clonk!* as the bathroom door high-fived my forehead, and I fell backward, unconscious. I awoke to a worried-stiff waiter, his watchful eyes looking over me. With dogged determination, I got to my feet and started muddling toward the bathroom. Evidently, I was out for just a second or two. Guille materialized in a flash and ushered me into the bathroom, assuring staff that he was a doctor and would give me medical attention. As he put my head down and applied refreshing, cold water to my face, the curtain lifted. Nausea and lightheadedness drifted away, and I was my old self again. Totally A-OK. In fact, I was fine enough to be able to return to the table to round off the meal without a hitch. Even Bill Belichick was none the wiser.

My uninvited maladies bid farewell as abruptly as they turned up. Bizarre.

As I gratefully enjoyed my renewed wellness, not to mention the remaining courses of our dinner, Guille pinpointed what transpired. My blood pressure, for some reason, had rapidly dropped. "And if anything like this ever happens again, just bend down and put your head on the table. We were actually in a booth, so you could have laid down there and felt better. Getting up actually made it worse," he helpfully advised.

Did you hear what he said? my brain asked. *You weren't imagining it at all. And if you hadn't ignored it, maybe you could have avoided all of this drama.*

Yeah, er, sorry about that, my mind gingerly owned up. *My mistake—I'll take your advice next time.*

As I played Monday-morning quarterback on what came about that night (and nursed my forehead's sore bump after that chummy encounter with the bathroom door), I marveled at how I kept downplaying what was going on. Just the same, it wasn't actually a mystery why I dismissed it all. In truth, the reason is pretty straightforward. Guille and I were having a superb time, scrumptious food surrounded us in a cushy establishment, and I didn't want anything to monkey with that. I mean, really. Who faints on her husband in a stylish dress at a fancy restaurant, on her birthday, of all days? The night just wasn't *supposed* to go that way. It's too random, and when it came to nipping *that* inconvenient randomness in the bud, my mind meant business. I reframed it, spun it, minimized it, disregarded it, and avoided it, right up until it landed me on the restaurant floor. What happened?

Denial is what happened, and—I can't emphasize this too much—we *all* do it. As a general rule, I'm not inclined to use absolute words like *all, none, always,* or *never,* but in a few cases I make an exception, and this is one of them. We *all* have a hodgepodge of tools we can use to ward off what we'd rather not face. And not only that, the art of escapism is peppered across the layers of human life. As my story makes clear, we can deny what's within us. But, as I said in the introduction, our talent at shirking the unpleasant fans out much farther, to our very identity, to our relationships with others and our life circumstances, to the society and culture we inhabit, and even to the more solemn issues of life and death. We'll be taking a guided tour of these layers in the coming chapters, but first, let's pause and get our bearings on what it is that we're really talking about here.

WHAT IS DENIAL?

According to Merriam-Webster, we've had *denial* in the English language for hundreds of years, and its definition illustrates the mixed bag of situations we can deny. Here are a few:

1. "refusal to acknowledge a person or a thing . . ."
2. "self-denial: denial of oneself: a restraint or limitation of one's own desires or interests"
3. "a psychological defense mechanism in which confrontation with a personal problem or with reality is avoided by denying the existence of the problem or reality"

Although the third definition presents denial more pointedly as a psychological defense, as we'll soon see, the refusal to acknowledge a person or thing, or not allowing yourself to do something you want, can also, arguably, be a means of defending ourselves.

Sigmund Freud, one of the most influential figures in the field of psychiatry, first put forward the image of denial as something we do to steer clear of thoughts that we don't want to admit to ourselves. Later, his daughter, Anna Freud, who went on to become a notable figure in her own right, was really the one who talked about denial as a psychological defense. She proposed that denial allows us to tweak our understanding of and perspective on an unsettling sphere of life that we'd rather avoid.[1] Now, even though I'm not exactly a Freud fan, I have to take my hat off to the Freuds for giving us the language to describe an all-too-human tendency to safeguard ourselves. When it comes to evading the unwanted in life, we humans are experts!

As the notion of denial moved forward in time from the Freuds' day, it became somewhat more controversial, with psychologists not exactly seeing eye to eye on how widely or narrowly to define it.[2] On this tour, we're going to view denial through a fuller lens in light of the science that points to denial's complex and multidimensional nature.[3]

So just how do we dodge the unseemly, exactly? If you're asking yourself this question right now, I'm there with you! *Denial* is, indeed, a broad term. In fact, when I think of denial, I envision one of those jumbo umbrellas, the kind that could shelter two people with room to spare for a third. Denial is the massive cover that shields us, and it's basically a way of turning down the dial (sometimes just barely; at other times, cranked all the way down) on what we don't want to deal with, either in ourselves, in others, or in the world around us. It's a suit of armor of sorts, designed to cushion us with protective insulation that gets puffed up or thinned out, depending upon our circumstances.

Yet, even as the strength of our armor changes, I think it's safe to say that we always have it on to some degree. At a minimum, we *always* have it at the ready, just in case we need it. And apparently we often do, as we seek out the sanctuary of escapism in all manner of life's nooks and crannies, from its gaping alcoves to its teeny crevices. Not only that, we possess an array of ways we can climb into these cozy hideouts. So with that in mind, what are some of the specific ways that we turn down the dial on what we don't want?

METHOD #1 OF TURNING DOWN THE DIAL: OUTRIGHT DENIAL

OK, let's start with the most straightforward method, where we can flat-out deny what's what with a "say it ain't so!" And the ground here is fertile indeed, as there is a bevy of "whats" that we can deny.[4] Even on the level of major life issues, the menu of what we can evade is long indeed. Here are just a few examples:

- an addiction we can't bring ourselves to acknowledge
- relationship troubles we'd rather not deal with
- thoughts and feelings after trauma that we're frightened to admit
- the sinking realization we'd rather not face that we've chosen the wrong career
- regret we're too guilt-ridden to admit about having children
- the need for help that we'd be ashamed to avow

Farther along the spectrum of facts we can deny, we come to the more day-to-day parts of life. Like that sniffle, tingly dry throat, and cough you're tending? No, that's not an impending cold that you have absolutely no time for! It's merely a case of allergies from the grassy, lush region you inhabit, right? (Never mind that it's winter and there's no pollen around.)

So, we can deny a wide range of facts. But if we were to group these into batches, what types of facts do we shirk?

Is it Pressing?

We can admit that there's an issue, but we deny that it's pressing or time sensitive. Procrastination is a prototypical illustration of this one. Sometimes the matters we put off are relatively trivial, like getting to the laundry tomorrow. At other times, our procrastination can be a bit more high-stakes. Take Fiona.

Like most of us, Fiona dreams up a whole collection of things she'd rather do than pay her bills. When the bills pile up on her kitchen counter, she pushes them out of her mind. It isn't until she learns that her delayed bill-paying has led to poor credit that she knows she can't push paying her bills to another day.

Does It Apply to Me?

We can also recognize an issue, but we tell ourselves that it just doesn't pertain to us.

Peter is a high-level, hardworking business consultant. Every night, after the stress of a long day, he has several drinks to unwind. When he's out with friends, he'll toss back a few more. At times, he wakes up with big blank patches from the night before, and the occasional weekend hangovers haven't been much fun either.

At his yearly checkup, Peter's physician cautions him about his drinking and the risks involved. "Sure, maybe I drink a little more than other people do, but most people don't have my workload. Otherwise, they'd be drinking more!" Peter nervously laughs. "Besides, if you're saying this could come back to bite me later, that's not happening. I've got this in check. I'm healthy, I'm probably getting promoted to partner, and I have a great life. Don't worry about me!"

Here we see that Peter is willing to admit that his alcohol use is heavier compared to other people, but he brushes off the idea that possible health problems from his alcohol use are relevant to him.

Am I Responsible for It?

Alternatively, we can admit that a problem exists but deny that we're responsible for addressing it.

Olive is struggling with depression, and she's feeling sort of stuck. Her therapist, Dr. Barrett, encourages her to take ownership of making changes that will improve her life and help her to feel better, but Olive denies that this is an issue for her to work out.

"Doc," Olive says, shaking her head, "I can't go out with friends, play my guitar, or work out when I'm feeling crummy. My depression won't let me. Besides, you're the therapist here. It's your job to do something and fix me!"

Notice that Olive acknowledges her struggle with depression but places the responsibility for lifting her depression and living a more gratifying life squarely on her therapist's shoulders, bypassing her pivotal, central part in it all.

Do I Feel It?

At times, we shrink from certain feelings because we believe it's unacceptable for us to experience them.

At the youthful age of twenty-eight, Malik is already a seasoned combat veteran, serving two tours in Iraq and one in Afghanistan. Since he came back to civilian life, fearfulness, a foreboding feeling, and sorrow continually follow him. Yet throughout his life and in the military, he got the unmistakable message that men don't get scared, they don't feel sad, and they can take charge of anything. Anger? Rage? Fine. He got that memo. But anything resembling fear or heartache? That is definitely not on the menu, and he does his best to fend any of that off. In his view, any man or soldier who feels fear, gets "the blues," or lets himself get overwhelmed by stuff is, well, just not fit to be either one.

In this example, Malik denies his feelings to himself. But it can go the other way too. We can don a façade, publicly disowning our emotions to others ("I'm doing great, thanks!" with a smile) even as we admit them to ourselves ("Ugh, I'm so miserable right now!").

Do I Think It?

Just as we can tag particular emotions as off-limits, we can give disconcerting thoughts the same treatment.

Victoria is a thirty-year-old pharmacist who does her utmost to be an open-minded, socially conscious, and caring individual. When she sees a woman in her sixties dressed in short shorts and a midriff-revealing tank top at the gym one day, she mumbles, "Ugh, really! Does she know how old she is? She's got the body, but it's still just gross!" A few weeks later, a well-meaning, trusted colleague pulls her aside and talks with her about her treatment of older customers. "Ageist!" Victoria sharply laughs and looks around, biting her lip. "You're telling me I'm ageist? I mean, thank you for talking to me, but that is utterly untrue. I fully believe that older people are just as capable as younger people and should be able to do whatever they want!"

For Victoria, the idea that she can hold prejudiced attitudes toward older individuals is just too unnerving, so she closes herself off to examining this possibility.

Although there is a medley of facts that we can deny, outright denial is not our only avenue for turning down the dial on what we don't want. We'll now look at how we use avoidance.

METHOD #2 OF TURNING DOWN THE DIAL: AVOIDANCE

Another way of eluding the elements of life we'd prefer not to see is to sidestep them—for real. Let's be honest here; sometimes ignorance is bliss and we just don't want the straight dope, do we? At times, we simply fancy a cocoon of naïveté, allowing us to protect ourselves from, well, *knowing* something. Let's turn to Tilly's story for a little more illumination.

Tilly is a thirty-seven-year-old administrative assistant at a large financial consulting firm, where a high-powered, frenzied atmosphere reigns. In her hope to earn a promotion, she volunteers to aid one of the firm's partners, Ms. Myers, serving as her right hand in wooing a financial heavyweight client. With grit and determination, Tilly clocks long hours with little sleep. Unfortunately, those three- to four-hour sleep sessions eventually backfire, giving birth to occasional errors. Tilly is petrified that the firm's CEO might let her go. On the morning of her performance review meeting, Tilly wakes with a cold dread. I just know they're going to demote me for those mistakes. Oh dear God, what if they sack me today? *Tilly sighs, frozen to her bed.* I seriously could not handle that! *Pausing, she grips her covers.* Ugh! I'm coming down with a baffling, twenty-first-century case of the Black Death. I just can't handle hearing "you're fired!" right now.

Although she doesn't *actually* know how the CEO will react, Tilly's choice to stay home shields her from the distressful feelings she dreads having to endure when she returns to work. It allows her to remain in the dark and, as far as she knows, remain among the employed for today, even if her boss gives her the sack tomorrow.[5]

Much as people tend to dodge facing the downer stuff, we steer clear of the cheery bottom line too. At first glance, that seems sort of peculiar but not when we zoom in on specific examples.[6] Have you ever tried to avoid hearing the plot for a movie or the ending of a show you've been dying to see? I know I have! And there are plenty of other ways we evade the upbeat:

- loved ones who keep mum about an upcoming party to avoid spoiling the surprise for the guest of honor
- couples who refuse to see each other in their wedding duds until the big day
- expectant parents who don't want to know the sex of their child until it's born

- eager eyes that swiftly dart away if they accidentally glimpse the end of that page-turner novel
- friends who draw out a captivating story to savor that deliciously hair-raising feeling of uncertainty and suspense

So far, we've been talking only about how we can steer clear of information, regardless of whether it's ugly or uplifting. But we're switch-hitters when it comes to avoidance, allowing us to do more than solely evade facts.[7]

Warding Off What It Means

We can take in the facts, but deftly veer away from putting them together and drawing broader conclusions about what they may painfully involve.

> *Erika loves her husband, Luke, deeply. Sadly, she notices that Luke seems uncommonly aloof, spends longer nights at the office, and guards his cell phone to a startling degree. The other night, she caught him texting someone in the middle of the night, but he staunchly denied it, claiming that he was just reading the news. And then, she takes his shirts to the dry cleaner and catches a whiff of someone else's perfume.* It's probably just a new cologne. He's working with important people, and he has to impress, *she tells herself.*

Despite her ability to acknowledge all of these pieces, Erika is unwilling to put them together and entertain the idea of an affair.

Cherry-Picking the Lowdown

Ready for some unwelcome news? Not everything we think is right is factual. Sometimes we nurse beliefs that miss the mark and misguide us. But the mere fact that our beliefs are off track at times doesn't stop us from stubbornly seeking whatever supports them, all the while pooh-poohing signs that we got it wrong. In other words, we cherry-pick what information we take in and what we toss to back up our own viewpoint. A more technical term for this is "selective exposure."[8]

Here's an illustration of this bias that I like to use with my classes. It's a fairly well-known stereotype that women are bad drivers, right? It's also the case that people who hold this view will be far more prone to look for, and ultimately notice, instances of women driving erratically. Supporting examples will seem to pop out at them, as if women are doling out driving goofs galore. And what of those women driving skillfully, or men driving in a grossly incompetent manner? In all likelihood, such counter-examples will either go unnoticed, or they'll be ripe for the kiss-off as exceptions to the rule: "Sure, maybe *she* drives well, but most women can't steer to save their lives!"

To recap, we can step away from what we don't want to see by avoiding facts themselves, by avoiding what they imply, or by being choosy with what information we look for, preferring to take in what bolsters our ideas and junk the rest.

Intriguingly, there are other methods of turning down the dial that are more like holding warm, fuzzy filters before our eyes, filters that help us migrate through life in a relatively more soothing, convenient, enjoyable way. They help to keep us snug as a bug in a rug—make that a soft, mega-plush rug. We'll explore two of those methods, self-enhancement and positive reinterpretation, in the following sections.

METHOD #3 OF TURNING DOWN THE DIAL: SELF-ENHANCEMENT

To be sure, the magician David Copperfield is an extraordinarily gifted illusionist, but the human mind's ability to conjure up perspectives that help us see elements of life in a softer light make him look like an amateur. Here, we'll pass through three main illusions that we use to embellish and elevate how we experience life.[9]

Mirror, Mirror on the Wall—I'm Quite Awesome!

The first illusion relates to how we see ourselves compared to other people. Let's take our personality, for example. If we were really being straight up with ourselves, we'd say that our personality is like a mixed bag of multicolored marbles. No one has an immaculate set. Some of the marbles are bright and lovely. Others are a bit duller with, eh, let's just say some nicks and a few scuffs. We all have virtues and shortcomings. It's part of being human!

And if someone asked you to rank your personality against the general population, where would you put yourself? In truth, if you're like most folks, you'll say that your temperament is more desirable than most. For example, in one study, 88 percent of people pegged their personality as being better than average.[10] The problem is that this cannot be true, as the average is usually in the middle range, around 50 percent. So, only about 50 percent of us can actually have a personality that's better than average, not 88 percent of us. But then, that's where positive illusions enter the scene. Even if we don't happen to be among those with an exceptional personality, we can certainly wend our way through life believing we are!

Don't Worry—I've Got This

The second type of illusion is about control. We certainly want to believe that we are able to wield control over the course of our fate. When I address this topic in class, I'll point out to my students that even though I *say* I'll see them next week, it's always possible that on the way home I could die in a car accident, through no fault of my own, never to see them again. Shocked faces stare at me, aghast, as if they never considered that my ability to see them next week was even in question, and it *could* be out of my control. I can always set my watch by those stunned, troubled faces. It's a human response to look at ourselves as commanding the driver's seat of life, mostly able to steer the course of our destiny.

I'll Take My Life Sunny-Side Up, Please

If you could look into a crystal ball that held an image of your future, what do you imagine you'd see? If you're like the majority of folks, you'll expect to see a buoyant, rosy image of the years ahead. As a matter of fact, most of us expect to have a shinier future compared to other people, by and large. However, just as most of us can't have a personality that's better than 50 percent of people, most of us can't have a future that's actually sunnier than the majority of other people. Nevertheless, as we walk forward into the unknown abyss of the future, it's useful to anticipate one that is full of promise. Just think, if you believed that gloom and unhappiness awaited you, would you conduct yourself differently than if you believed that you were advancing toward joy and fulfillment? I don't want to speak for you, but personally, I'm betting that you would.

Does any of this mean that you don't actually have a peachy personality, the ability to choose and influence events in your life, or a smashingly bright future before you? Absolutely not. This could really all be true! It just means that there are more elements in life that are out of our control than we think, and it's not possible for *all* of us to have personalities and futures that outrank the ones of most other folks.

All that said, it really doesn't matter where our personality or life technically ranks. We're all works in progress, and what's truly important is that we're living a life that's meaningful, enjoyable, and rewarding to us, regardless of how we stack up against others. And if there's one thing we can control, it's how we choose to see what happens in life. This brings me to our final tool in our turn-down-the-dial kit.

METHOD #4 OF TURNING DOWN THE DIAL: POSITIVE REINTERPRETATIONS

When we positively reinterpret a situation, we're essentially throwing a different color light on it.[11] Here's a classic case of "putting a new frame on a picture."

One spring morning, Lily walks to work wearing lovely new white pants. When a bus splashes headlong into a humongous muddy puddle, bathing Lily in mahogany-colored H_2O, she doesn't stomp her foot and curse her unhappy lot of having to go to work with mud all over her, although this would be an understandable reaction. Instead she thinks about the sheer randomness of it, and the irony that it happened, of all days, when she was wearing new white pants. She envisions how comedic this must have looked and throws back her head in laughter.

The crux of this is that humor wasn't inherently built into that event. It only became hysterical because of the way Lily framed it in her mind. Her perspective transformed what could have been a highly upsetting moment into an entertaining story to tell her friends.

And it's not hard to find heaps of other examples in life. Do any of these look familiar? If none of them do, that's alright. See if you can think of any others that fit your own life.

- You look back on a painful time in the past and realize you were glad it happened because you grew in unbelievable ways. It could be an addiction you're recovering from, an abusive relationship you got out of, or emotional pain from your past that you dealt with.
- You face a hefty challenge and remind yourself that you've overcome greater ones. Your challenge could be an overwhelming project at work or school, a momentous change in life that you're tackling, or a personally

difficult but aspirational goal you've set for yourself, such as finishing a marathon.

- You transform a frustrating experience into a more tolerable, if not gratifying, one. An example of this would be getting irritated about being in gridlock traffic, then seeing it as an opportunity to practice a presentation for work or simply reflect on life.
- You find that you can't afford to upgrade your house to something larger, as you'd hoped, but choose to see extraordinary good fortune all around you by appreciating what you have, and the people and things you encounter every day. It might be your partner whom you treasure, giving thanks for having such a special person in your life. Maybe you appreciate your ability to move your body the way you want to, or sleep with a roof over your head. Perhaps you envision the sky and stars as beautiful gifts for you to see.

Of course, there are limits to what positive reframing can do. It won't magically wipe away stress, anger, sadness, grief, or fear, nor should it. Painful stuff happens in life, plain and simple. We can't just snap our fingers and, with a reframe, banish the pain of losing a spouse, a friend, or a child. Yet it's also true that, in many situations, we have room to view events in our life through a fresh, more sublime lens.

Yes, we certainly have diverse byways that we can use to swerve from what fills us with unease. We can outright deny, avoid, self-enhance, or positively reframe. Not only that, we have discrete reasons for steering clear in the first place. Let's check out three that psychology researchers point to.[12]

WHY WE TURN DOWN THE DIAL

In this section, we'll look at three common reasons we turn down the dial on what we don't want to look at full in the face.

To Tone Down an Upsetting Feeling or Hold On to a Pleasurable One

Did you ever tell your friends not to give away the season finale of your favorite show because you had it recorded at home and were aching to watch it later? Chalk it up to your attempt to savor the fun-filled tension and sense of surprise for yourself. Or remember how Tilly played sick from work? Part of her reason for calling in ill was to spare herself, even for one day, the emotional anguish she anticipated if her boss were to let her go. The long and short of it is that, every so often, we evade what we don't want to look at to manage our emotions.

To Cling to Viewpoints That We Hold Dear

On occasion, we do not lay eyes on a matter because it would involve altering important beliefs about ourselves, other people, or the world around us. That was true of Erika, the loving wife who couldn't bring herself to even consider that her husband, Luke, was having an affair. If she were to explore this issue and discover an affair, she might have to let go of her cherished notion that she is in a loyal, dependable marriage and that her husband is true-blue. Or, perhaps like Peter in his response to his doctor's concern about his alcohol intake, we've always believed that we had a handle on our drinking, and so we steer away from taking a good, honest look at how and why we drink. Alternatively, we might depend upon the notion that we can control our fate, unable to grapple with the fact that we're a bit more vulnerable than we realize.

To Maintain the Status Quo of How We Live

Finally, there are occasions when taking the bull by the horns means we'll have to make unappealing, inconvenient choices in life or face a consequence that we have absolutely no taste for. To protect ourselves from change, we skip out on dealing with certain hard truths. For example, if we don't acknowledge that we made the wrong career choice, then we won't feel bound to make a dramatic about-face. We won't have to make less than desirable lifestyle changes if we don't keep that doctor's appointment and discuss our health. If we hoodwink ourselves that we're only doing fun, sociable drug use, rather than battling an addiction, we can cushion ourselves from giving up a comforting, albeit destructive, habit.

Thus far we've explored a potpourri of ways we run for cover from the undesirable, as well as some of our reasons for doing it. As we edge toward the conclusion of this part of the tour, I hope it's clear that denial is wide-ranging in the purposes that it serves and the roles that it plays in our lives. Notably, some of these roles are quite useful, even healthful!

WHY TURNING DOWN THE DIAL ISN'T ALWAYS A BAD THING

It's awfully regrettable that denial gets the bad, pathological rap that it does. True, we can guard and insulate ourselves in ways that are unhealthy and ultimately work against us. Taking time to collect ourselves before reading what we foresee will be a heartbreaking email or letter can lend us the emotional preparation we need, but refusing to ever open it may be a decision we'll regret later.[13] Similarly, if we decide not to go back for the results of our HIV test because we fear the outcome, this is unhelpful, not to mention potentially life-threatening.[14] And yet, between 12 and 55 percent of people who take an HIV test do not return for the results.[15]

Life problems that we won't deal with or an unworkable relationship that we turn a blind eye to are additional examples.

On the other hand, as I mentioned, it's equally true that turning down the dial can be helpful and psychologically healthy. It's an essential facet of life that helps us feel our best and flourish while we're taking care of the business of living. It lends time to emotionally prepare ourselves before we attend to what distresses us. It paints a challenging matter in hues that offer relief and that help us marshal needed strength as we cope. It hands us a sense of control and the anticipation of a sparkling future, all of which impart a greater sense of security, calm, and spiritedness as we march into the murkiness of an unforeseeable future. Arguably, this emboldens us to make levelheaded decisions and lionhearted changes as we go.

So the long and short of it is that, if I could shout anything about denial through a bullhorn, it would be this:

Don't ditch denial—just have a healthy relationship with it!

As we journey forward together to the exercises at the end of this chapter, and then on through the varied realms of denial, I'm knocking on wood that you'll be ready and willing to acknowledge when you're using denial in a less than healthy manner. Trust me, it won't mean that you're flawed, broken, strange, or impaired. The key is to learn when denial is working for us and when it's not. If it's useful for you and is furnishing you with a better quality of life, by all means, keep it around! And in those spaces where you find it's taking more from you than it's giving, kick it to the curb and pick up another tool. It's kind of like the joke about the guy who goes into his doctor.

Guy: "Doctor, it hurts when I lift my arm!"

Doctor: "So don't lift your arm!"

Throughout this book, there's going to be zero judgment from me in how you turn down the dial. I'm also assuming that you're an intelligent, competent, well-intentioned person who is capable of making your own decisions and sorting through what feels right for you in your life. I'm going to walk beside you, sorting through the ways denial emerges across our lives and the assorted ways it can elevate or hinder us. To put it another way, I'm going to invite you here and there to try lifting your arm and seeing what happens. Are you ready to move forward? OK, let's go to the first set of exercises!

EXERCISES

Exercise 1: Getting Clear on Steering Clear

We all have a rich personal history in which we encountered messages about denial, probably saw models of how other people used denial, and had firsthand experiences with using it ourselves. In this exercise, you will have an opportunity to take a clearer look at the origins of your perspective on denial. Please take a separate sheet, paper or digital, and fill in the following sentences. If you can, try not to overthink them. There are no right or wrong answers. Just fill in what feels most truthful for you. If you don't know how to answer, that's OK too. In that case, leave it blank and come back to it later.

1. While I was growing up, if my caregivers had given me instructions on how to use denial, they would have advised me to __________.
2. Over the course of my life, the kinds of messages about denial that I got from role models, friends, and society at large included __________.
3. Overall, there was __________ denial in my family. (Pick one of the following to fill in the blank: *no, a little, some, a lot of,* or *total.*)
4. The kinds of denial I tend to use are __________.
5. If I could wave a magic wand and put myself in denial about anything, it would be __________.
6. When I think about the times when denial has worked well for me, what comes to mind is __________.

7. When I think about the times when denial hasn't worked well for me, what comes to mind is __________.

Exercise 2: Finding Your Purpose

We all have our own reasons for wanting to explore denial and figure out the ways it impairs us, as well as how it lends us a hand. When we're plugged into our sense of purpose—the "whys" behind what we're doing—it's invaluable. Like a guiding star, purpose directs us toward where we're heading, rather than allowing us to meander off in directions less likely to give us the results we want. This exercise will help you make out your own "whys" and sense of purpose for learning about the role of evasion in your life. Please take a separate sheet and write down your answers to each of the following questions. If the answers don't come to you right away, that's fine. Be patient with yourself and take your time. Let the questions percolate over a refreshing walk outside, a soothing bath, a little tea, or some relaxing music. You don't have to answer them in one day either. Take all the time you need.

1. What kind of book was I looking for when I came across this one?
2. When I saw this book, what were my first thoughts?
3. When I took a look at it, what was it about the book that popped out at me and made me decide to buy it?
4. When I looked at the list of chapters, which one(s) really hit home for me?
5. Is there anything going on in my life right now that made me want to read this book? If so, what?
6. What are the three things I'm most hoping to get out of reading this book? (P.S. If there are more than three things, you're welcome to list those too!)
7. When I'm being as honest with myself as I can be, what is my biggest overall hope for what I want my life to look like as a result of reading this book?

2

DENIAL WITHIN US

"I wasn't crying about mothers," he said rather indignantly. "I was crying because I can't get my shadow to stick on. Besides, I wasn't crying."

—J. M. Barrie, *Peter Pan*

If you feel vulnerable and alone with invisible woes and fruitless efforts to dodge the feelings and thoughts that disquiet you and push your buttons, you're not alone. Jasper's story is a case in point.

Whuff, *the sofa cushion salutes Jasper as he sits across from his therapist, Dr. Morales.*

"It's ridiculous," Jasper huffs. "I just feel miserable, and I can't make it stop. Everyone else just seems so positive and at peace, and I'm the freakish odd one out who's not happy."

Dr. Morales pauses, an empathetic sigh breaking the silence. "It must be so daunting to think that the rest of the world holds a secret that you don't, and that no matter how hard you try to stop feeling what you do, everything stalls."

"Yes!" Jasper says. "I keep telling myself to stop being such a wishy-washy twit, sitting in the dumps. I try so hard to ram it down and pretend I don't feel what I do, but nothing works."

"Uh, forgive me, but could we take a step back?" Dr. Morales calmly asks. "Before you started trying to hold off your sadness, did you find out what left you feeling sad in the first place?"

"What?" Jasper asks, befuddled. "You mean, just let myself feel sad?"

"Yeah," Dr. Morales says. "Did you ever allow yourself to feel sad without trying to fend it off and see what happened next?"

"Hah," Jasper half-laughs, "No, why would I want to do that? If I let myself feel sad, then it's just gonna stick around and I'll feel worse. What's the point of that?"

"Maybe," Dr. Morales suggests, "the sadness is stuck because you're trying to push it away?"

"Oh no, this is crazy," Jasper moans, then points at his therapist, "and you're crazy. What you're telling me makes no sense, and this therapy isn't working anyway. I think we're done here."

Screech, *the bar stool welcomes Jasper in a chummy fashion.*

"Hey, Jasper!" Charlie hails from behind the bar. "Want your usual?"

"Come hell or high water, my friend! Let the pouring begin!"

Like a lot of folks, Jasper seemed sure that if he could just be little a more effective at evading his feelings and thoughts, his troubles would fade away. Truthfully, in the world of emotional escapism, there are legions of Jaspers.

To the eye, it makes splendid sense why we would think that shirking unwanted internal experiences is the ticket. After all, if you suddenly found yourself standing near a scorching fire in a building, I'll bet you wouldn't be there for long. It's all too human to seek out what feels agreeable and skip out on what feels cruddy. To be sure, the "draw near what's good, ditch what's bad" blueprint is a loyal friend to us in a zillion ways. On the other hand, that recipe sometimes ricochets on us, including in the world of our inner life.

That brings us to the first stop on our tour: denial within us. We'll peruse denial of physical pain and illness. Then we'll burrow into our efforts to wriggle away from feelings that we don't want and hold them in darkness. At the same time, we'll probe how turning down the dial on our inner experience lends an essential hand to lift us up in times of need. Then we'll delve into how we aren't nearly as in-the-know about our mind-set as we'd like to assume. Finally, exercises at the close of the chapter will offer chances to put some of what we've explored into practice in your own life.

Are you ready to take a hard look at the many ways we escape our inner discomfort? If you're like most folks, you have a wavering reaction to that question. "Yes, I am, let's do this!" versus "Uh, wait, maybe I don't really want to know!" And that's just fine. It's what being human is about! So as we tread onward, please know that you control the pace of the journey we'll be taking in this chapter. Our digestion of denial is most likely going to involve *some* unpleasantness. After all, we're flying in the face of avoidance. Yet, as we'll notice time and again during our journey together, life is about balance. Our tour of evasion calls for pathways that are rugged and uphill to some degree, but ultimately wholesome and passable. With that said, let's get started.

LET'S GET PHYSICAL . . . OR NOT

Alas, if you're human, it's pretty certain that your body is going to hurt from time to time. And let's face it: Pain is a pain! Sadly, many folks deal with pain a lot of the time, if not all of the time. But even if your pain isn't chronic, in all likelihood you can tell between types of pain. We can have cramps, aches, spasms, throbs, or soreness, not to mention stings, twinges, stitches, cricks, pangs, irritations, and burns. Is it a "sharp" or a "dull" pain? Most of us know exactly what that means. Yet, in spite of the fact that we share similar language for pain, our experience of it is decidedly personal, as is our choice of how we're going to manage it.

Thankfully, it turns out that we're capable of managing pain more than we realize. In a 2015 study, volunteers tried to visualize painful heat as being either less or more intense than it felt. And it worked.[1] We're able to modulate pain up or down with our mind. We experience discomfort through our pain receptors, as well as regions of our brain related to sizing up how we feel and the situations we're in. Even though we can't actually alter our own pain receptors, we can mentally soothe discomfort through our brain's other pain escape hatch: denial. In essence, we can mentally hoodwink ourselves into experiencing less pain and buy into our self-deception in the process. Not bad! What's more, cutting-edge virtual reality treatment is now on hand that offers folks a technological boost in mentally diverting their attention away from pain, in effect turning down the dial on their bodies to ease what hurts.[2]

Your Body Is a Super-Chatty Friend—Listen to It

At the same time, there are limits to the advantages of being disconnected from our body. For instance, another 2015 study supports the health perks of being plugged in to our body and its messages for our well-being.[3] Specifically, people who are attuned to their body's physical signals are more content with how their body looks, and they feel more self-assured in their own skin compared to folks with a duller connection to their bodies. What's more, they shoulder fewer health worries, and they enjoy better sexual satisfaction and sexual self-esteem. So even though it can behoove us to turn down the dial on our awareness, we don't want to turn it down to such an extent that we pass over valuable tip-offs from our body.

Our mind is a powerful force for pain management, indeed. At the same time, we ought to be cautious about how distant we get from our body's tidings; they're pivotal for our quality of life. Coming up, we'll make one more physical stop: veering away from physical illness.

Intruders in the Skin We Live In

There's no space more private, no nook that is more uniquely ours in every respect, than our own body. It's our home. It's an integral part of what makes us, well, us. And we're accustomed to ruling it, aren't we? It's ironic, then, that the space where we face the greatest hazards is in our own being, where microscopic burglars and turncoats invade the home that is our body. Meg found that out in a dramatic fashion.

> *On Tuesday morning as Meg wakes and mindlessly puts a hand on her face, her fingers do a double-take and she bolts from bed as she feels the left side of her face is puffed out. Her jaw drops open as she sees the bulging mass there.*
>
> *When her trusty physician, Dr. Walters, walks into the room for her appointment later that day, his mouth falls open in fascination at the now dramatically enlarged mound. "Wow! That's unbelievable!" he exclaims. "You've got one hell of an infection, Meg," Dr. Walters observes, examining her. "You're lucky that antibiotics exist, because we're going to need to give you some heavy-duty ones for this."*

These little miniscule thingamabobs can take our body hostage at their whim and pull us down. And it doesn't take a whole lot to crush us. Even that relatively meek pest, the common cold, has the power to take us down at least a peg or two. According to the Centers for Disease Control and Prevention, colds have the oddball badge of honor of being the top reason why we call in sick from work or school.[4] But what about dire ailments, such as various forms of cancer, Alzheimer's disease, or HIV? These conditions touch countless people around the world. It's here where we now turn.

Despite denial's history of infamy as an unhealthy coping strategy, a multitude of psychologists (including this one) believe that denial can actually be a healthful, well-adjusted way of dealing with a major illness.[5] Consider cancer, for instance. Over one hundred million Americans face a cancer diagnosis every year. Denial of cancer does not have to mean that the people diagnosed with it must unceasingly pretend they're in sterling health. They can acknowledge their battle with cancer and still employ denial from time to time to make it through.[6] A cancer diagnosis and the possible implications of it are mind-boggling and are bound to unleash tidal waves of immense emotion. Even though it's pivotal to face momentous truths like a life-threatening or terminal illness, at times we also need to take such information in small doses.

Turning down the dial on what we don't want can also be a right-minded game plan in the face of chronic illness. For instance, as we age, we're prone to becoming more solitary as we battle chronic ailments.[7] But a 2015 study out of Concordia University revealed that older adults who use positive reinterpretation to cope with chronic illness are more safeguarded from the same, lonely fate.[8]

And an earlier study showed that older adults recuperating from a major health condition who used denial to cope were more liable to be back in business and reconnected with their daily lives. What's more, they could acknowledge the reality of their condition and still use denial. If we zoom in a little more closely, we'll see that at least some of their denials will pretty likely remind you of the positive reinterpretation we covered in the previous chapter. For instance, several people stacked up the hardships of their illness against their traumatic childhoods, which they viewed as being far more challenging, or as giving them the know-how to handle their physical condition in the present day. When they painted their illness in *that* light, it didn't seem as terrible.[9] We're seeing a theme here: It looks like it's truly possible to use denial *and* be sensible, mature, and well-adjusted at the same time.

Be that as it may, our choice to turn down the dial on a disquieting, naked truth comes with thistles from time to time, ready to lance us. Denial can be rather destructive if we use it to shield ourselves too heavily. Take coronary artery disease, for example. It's the number one cause of death among older women, making it a paramount health issue for us all to think about, whether we're a woman or we love someone who is. And what gets in the way of people being able to get a handle on this disease? Here's a hint: It starts with a D. In effect, denial is so potent that it stands as one of the supreme roadblocks to conquering one of our most lethal public health issues.[10]

Denial also drives another immense public health problem: HIV and AIDS. A 2014 study in Tanzania, Africa, for example, revealed that denial, as well as the social shame that people tag onto themselves for being HIV positive, predicts a lower likelihood of following HIV treatment recommendations.[11] That shame has proven to be universal. In the public mind, this disease is tied so closely to reckless sexual behavior that the stigma keeps people who have contracted it in other ways from getting tested.

To sum up, denial and other approaches to turning down the dial work for us brilliantly, especially when we're forced to square off against serious health conditions. Then, at other times, they curb our wherewithal to suitably look after our well-being. Thus far we've been talking about the physical realm. In this next bend in the road on our trek, we'll touch on the world of emotions.

THE TIDE OF OUR EMOTIONS

If the idea of delving into our avoidance of feelings leaves you a bit spooked, that's totally understandable. Depending on the emotions we're dealing with, they can be awfully distressing, and it makes good sense not to want to feel them. I mean, do you know anyone who jumps up excitedly, waving their arms about, for a shot at sticking their hands in scalding water? At times in life, agonizing emotions don't seem all that different from the pain of a second-degree burn.

And yet it's also true that we sometimes run for cover from unnerving feelings, fearful they'll smother us, when in point of fact they're advantageous to us, even if unpleasant. It reminds me of a framed picture of a shark that I recently received. This shark is humongous and menacing, with massive, knifelike teeth stretching widely below seemingly hollow, frosty eyes. As terrorizing as this shark appears, in reality it's a sand tiger shark—a timid, meek, placid creature.[12] It's a reminder that not all of what we fear and avoid is sinister or destructive. Time and again, plenty of what we turn away from is, well, a lamb in shark's clothing.

It's a tightrope walk as we avert the unwanted. On the one hand, if we lean too far to the left for too long, then we're habitually disconnecting from our inner world, and we lose out on invaluable information that can actually lend us a hand. On the other hand, if we lean too far to the right for too long, then we're stewing and simmering in our emotions. For the most part, people do their level best to turn down the dial on undesirable feelings, especially if the feelings are unhelpful to them.[13] Ultimately, balance is the key. Consider Una's situation.

> *Una is in a large formal meeting at work when her boss makes a comment that peeves her.*
>
> Ugh! I can't believe he just took credit for Gerald's idea! He's got no shame whatsoever, *she fumes to herself. Yet she soon realizes that this emotion won't serve her in the moment. This situation calls for coolness and attention to detail, so she gives it her best shot to turn down the dial on her exasperation.*
>
> Una, you have more important things to focus on right now, *she silently reminds herself.* This project is what matters, and you can always think about your boss later, *she thinks as she takes slow breaths.*
>
> *As she feels the tension leave her body, her focus returns to the meeting.*

By the same token, if it looks as if an emotion is giving you a signal that there's something you legitimately need to address, then it is healthier to come closer to it than to dial it down.[14] Let's return to Jasper, who was desperately unhappy. His psychologist, Dr. Morales, tried to get him to attend to his sadness so he could figure out why he felt down. After all, Jasper's melancholy likely reflects valuable information about an aspect of his life that's hurtful, such as an unmet need or a loss. Similar to a well-functioning fire alarm in a building, emotions can be extremely unpleasant, but many a time, there's actually a crucial message coming to you that you probably don't want to miss.

In essence, emotional evasion has two sides. One side is alluring for sure but ultimately harmful. It's a strategy that robs us of far more than it lays at our feet, as in Jasper's case. The other is a tried-and-true sidekick, at the ready to help us delay or put aside actions that might be inappropriate or self-defeating, as we saw with Una. Let's explore these two faces of denial in more depth.

A DELIGHTFUL MOUSETRAP—ONLY WE'RE THE MOUSE

On the face of things, doesn't it just seem like the answer to disagreeable feelings is to run for cover to our bat cave, where they can't pester us anymore? It seems so logical. The trouble is that we don't quite operate that way. Ironically, recent research reveals that the more we ward off bothersome emotions on a day-to-day basis, the more the unpleasant feelings dwell within us and the more the pleasurable ones seem further out of reach.[15] What's more, evasion of our inner world is connected to emotional collapse and burnout at work.[16]

Believe it or not, we can avoid heartening, hopeful feelings too. Cheerfulness, contentment, love, or bliss can feel unnerving for some folks. Unfortunately for them, feeling good may be accompanied by a sense of dread, which ties in with emotional angst, nervous tension, and misery.[17] One possible reason some people evade buoyant feelings is to lessen the odds that, just when they're feeling cheerful, life will hand them a bitter pill, forcing them to plummet in an emotional letdown. Just imagine you were convinced you were going to fall. Wouldn't you rather tumble from a low place so you couldn't get scraped quite as much?[18] Sadly, by trying to protect ourselves from disappointment, we are likely to end up feeling more disappointed with our life without joy.

Running for Cover after Trauma

The more we shun our painful feelings in the wake of a trauma such as a car accident, rape, or combat, the more likely we are to bump into stumbling blocks on the road to emotional healing, leaving us more at risk for grappling with post-traumatic stress symptoms (e.g., staying away from anything that reminds you of the trauma, feeling tightly wound, having difficulty sleeping, being easily startled).[19] Yet it's beyond understandable why anyone would steer clear of such feelings. That's one of the umpteen reasons why I hold great respect and admiration for people who give therapy a try. Let's be honest, it can be intimidating, unnerving, and just plain scary to reach out for help. It's totally bold and courageous to abandon the apparent safety of living with the symptoms and face the trauma that is causing them. Many people try to continue skipping out on their feelings in therapy, and even though I utterly get why they do this, it's also more likely to keep folks from making headway in working through their pain.[20]

Sidestepping into Addiction

Addiction, both to compulsive behaviors and mood-altering substances, is another domain where emotional avoidance and psychological hardship traipse hand in hand.

For example, when we evade unwanted experiences inside us, we're also more prone to grapple with harmful levels of gambling,[21] which, sadly, offers the promise of feelings—like excitement, hope, and happiness—that can provide temporary solace from the real feelings of boredom, hopelessness, and sadness that a person experiences. But we don't have to spend money to fend off burdensome feelings. There's also a link between our drive to bypass unsettling emotions and Internet addiction, particularly in the form of online gaming.[22] Does this mean that if you're a gamer, you must be warding off vexing feelings? Absolutely not! Plenty of people play for the sheer pleasure of it, similar to folks who let loose with the occasional game of blackjack or a few rounds at the slot machine. As long as we have a healthy relationship with gambling or the Internet, we're cool.

In the world of substance addiction, emotional escapism rips us off with a smile too. For instance, a 2015 psychological research study from the University of Texas Medical School at Houston shows that people who stay away from their inner experiences related to cocaine use (such as their feelings) are less likely to stay on track with treatment for cocaine dependence, even when that treatment is well-researched and quite potent.[23] In fact, it's a truism that substance misuse is a way of "medicating" uncomfortable feelings and that not wanting to face those feelings is a key dynamic in not admitting you have problem with alcohol or other drugs. "He's in denial," is a common plaint of both family members and counselors regarding people with addiction disorders in general.

The fact that the majority of therapists admit to being unclear on how to effectively treat someone with denial speaks to its knotty, intricate nature.[24] Undoubtedly, though, the prospect of releasing denial, admitting to a problem with substances, and letting go of the very thing that offers protection from formidable feelings is thorniest for the person in the grip of addiction. In the course of my work, I've had the privilege of walking side by side with numerous people as they explored the role of alcohol and other drugs in their lives. And although their stories are unique, an intertwining theme is the utter humanness of wanting to evade deep unhappiness, anguish, or heartache (to name a few emotions), and to reach for a remedy to take these feelings away. Alongside this understandable drive, other hopes fall in, such as wanting to make life a little more bearable or to feel a little numb inside in order to continue functioning on a day-to-day basis. The tricky catch with this solution is that it works—in the short run. It numbs, enlivens, soothes, or distracts, or all of the above.

Maybe the emotions are so overwhelming that it feels like they will never stop if they aren't nailed down with *something*.

Or perhaps alcohol and other drugs seem like the only option to cope with unalterable circumstances, such as living in a theater of war, extreme poverty, or an abusive family. But regardless of what ground substance addiction springs from, what makes it especially cruel is that it gives with one hand in the beginning and takes with both hands later. Not only does it stop working, it blocks the ability to heal the very emotions that drive the addiction, and it tends to create new painful experiences on top of everything else. But in the midst of addiction, denial can be a thick cloak that protects from the downsides of dependence. For anyone with a problem with alcohol or other drugs, I recognize and respect the struggle between continuing what feels safe and familiar, and discarding denial. Yet, as risky as it feels to let denial go, the most profound hazard is holding on to it. I've witnessed firsthand the personal vigor and wholeness that infuses people who ditch denial and the false sanctuary of mood-altering substances and, as a result, come up to meet themselves.

The gist here is that emotional evasion, particularly when it's chronic, doesn't ensnare us in agony *despite* our best shot at fending off emotions, but precisely *because* of the dodging we're doing. On the other hand, turning down the dial doesn't always boomerang on us.

THE UPSIDES IN SCALING DOWN

All of us, for all intents and purposes, will be hurt in a relationship (with relatives, friends, partners, and so on) at some point in our lifetime, which means that we'll also have to grapple with the question of whether to eventually forgive another person in order to get past that hurt and move on. Now, forgiveness is an emotionally charged issue, and it's not for me to tell you whether or when you might need to forgive someone. But if we do decide to forgive and soothe nagging, hurtful feelings—regardless of whether we wish to maintain a connection with that person or not—when we give ourselves the opportunity to reframe our perspective toward that person in a more charitable light, we're more apt to feel an increase in pleasant feelings, along with a boost in compassion for the person who wronged us.[25]

Reframing our emotions can also be useful when we have to decide if our nervousness over facing a challenge in our lives will be experienced as debilitating anxiety or if it can be reframed as excitement and channeled as positive energy for completing the task.

Those Jittery Butterflies

Let's say you've been chosen to make a presentation at a conference for work, and as the date approaches, your nervousness increases. When the day finally arrives, as you wait to give your speech, your heart starts to race, your breathing increases, you get butterflies in your stomach, and you feel a jittery energy. Does this sound like nervousness to you, or excitement? It all hinges on how you reframe the arousal in your body. If you tell yourself that you're feeling excitement, then you're more apt to feel excited, and this translates into doing a better job of giving the speech.[26] It reminds me of a fabulous saying: "It's alright to have butterflies in your stomach. Just get them to fly in formation."[27] If you can reframe that stirring feeling in your body as excited energy, then it can become a friend that helps you give a more energetic, dynamic speech. Luckily, if you want to learn to touch up your frame of reference in a bright, fresh way, there's no secret to it. Practice is the name of the game. A 2015 study shows that when we practice reframing we're more inclined to manage bothersome feelings in an effective way.[28]

What We Don't Buy

People are highly disposed to safeguard themselves from losses, including financial ones.[29] Whenever we have to tighten our monetary belts and scratch an item off our shopping list, it hurts. It's not fun to walk by that slightly pricier but oh-so-delicious cereal you love while reminding yourself that you can't afford to buy it anymore. One study demonstrated that when our budget decreases, we prefer to buy a more limited range of products than we did before, cutting some items off of our shopping list completely, rather than spending less across multiple kinds of items. For example, let's say that you would typically buy three frozen pizzas, eight pink lady apples, two tubs of cottage cheese, two containers of salad greens, one box of instant oatmeal, a gallon of orange juice, a loaf of bread, and two cartons of almond milk. If you suddenly got a raise, you might find yourself branching out and adding a little variety to your shopping list, like blueberries or carrot juice. But if unexpected expenses came your way and suddenly you had a more limited budget, then you would be more inclined to scale back your purchasing variety. And why? We tend to believe that if we eliminate a few items from our list (e.g., the pizzas and the cottage cheese), rather than spend just a little less across everything, we buy (e.g., four apples instead of eight, one container of greens instead of two, etc.), then we can cushion ourselves from distressing feelings of loss after a fiscal hit by not having to slash our budget as many times.[30] Thus, our drive to turn down our internal dial not only has psychological effects, but economic ones too.

To recap, as much as it's understandable and human to want to hold agonizing parts of our inner world at bay, by and large this comes back to whack us down, leaving us stranded in the ooze of our own misery. On the other hand, when the goggles we use to see our world and ourselves get a little fine-tuning, we can turn down the dial on undesirable feelings in a fashion that elevates the caliber of our life. Notice that these are all ways we navigate our relationship to our inner world. But what about the ways in which our inner world influences us without us even realizing it?

SHADOWY PUPPET MASTERS

On the whole, we like to think we're in the know when it comes to our attitudes and what impacts our decisions. And even though, many a time, we are plugged in to our emotional life and why we do what we do, it's also true that something else is oftentimes pulling the strings outside of our awareness. Now, to be sure, I'm not trying to say that we aren't actually making our own choices. But I *am* saying that unobservable influences bear upon what we choose in virtually every aspect of life. For instance, we all hold attitudes that we don't even realize we have, yet they impact our reactions and decisions nonetheless. So, as we near the conclusion of this stop on our tour, we'll peruse some of the ways in which hidden factors influence our viewpoints and deeds, despite our desire to cling to the idea that we're the ones running our own show. In fact, on this segment of our journey we're going to take a more panoramic perspective and spotlight our denial of this naked truth: We're not pulling our own strings or running our own show as much as we'd like to think we are. The themes to follow reflect assorted illustrations that whittle away at this denial, bringing the terra firma of truth to light.

Our Shrouded Take on the Sun

Perhaps one of the most fundamental and important choices we face pertains to how we treat our body. Ordinarily, it feels like we're the ones driving those choices, but there's a little more under the hood of our health habits than we comprehend. Take how much we expose ourselves to the sun, for instance. When you read the word *tan,* what comes to mind? Do you envision bronzed, sun-soaked, coconut-oiled skin speckled with sand on a fun-filled beach day? Does the word seem irrelevant because you have more melanin in your skin and don't think about tanning much because your skin is already darker? Or do you picture sunspots, skin cancer, and premature wrinkles? Regardless of what pops up for you consciously, these ideas likely aren't primarily driving what you do once you're outside. A University of Florida study revealed that it's actually our latent, unconscious attitudes about basking in the sun that best forecast whether and how much we tan.[31] When we hold favorable implicit attitudes toward tanning, then we're more apt to do it and in potentially harmful ways.[32] But, even if we have a positive unconscious attitude, we can strive to compensate by being more watchful of our sun habits and prevent burning or, worse, skin cancer.

The Unseen Side of What We Eat

Another crucial health decision we make every day is what we choose to eat. But how aware are we of what goes into our nutritional decisions? Eh, not as much as we may think. Unobservable, implicit attitudes toward different kinds of foods sway our choices. A 2014 study showed that when people had favorable unconscious associations with fruit, they were twice as inclined as people with neutral associations to choose fruit over a granola snack when given the choice. And they were three times more apt to select fruit than the folks with a negative unconscious attitude toward nature's candy.[33]

So what do you do if you want to give your food repertoire an upgrade? Shine a little more awareness on your emotions.[34] We have potent emotional responses to food (the next time you're out to dinner, look around and check how you and other folks respond to the dinner and dessert menus). Additionally, we can make food choices in reaction to particular feelings. "Stress eating" is a classic example of this.[35] In a 2015 study, people received training to enhance their emotional awareness and capacity to eat in a more observing, mindful manner. Not only did they eat healthier, but they lost more weight in three months, even more than folks who received information about nutrition and healthy food choices.[36] So, if you want to enhance your lifestyle and eat a little healthier, consider paying more attention to your emotions while you're poring over nutritional info. This may be an even more potent pathway toward a healthier you.

The Covert Influence of Addiction

Unobservable influences also impact addiction and the pathway toward recovery. For instance, science suggests that folks who are addicted to alcohol or other drugs can pay attention to drinking or drug use, even before they consciously realize it.[37] In other words, people grappling with addiction can find their minds turned toward alcohol or another drug of choice against their will, and this can continue even after they are sober.[38] And it makes sense why this happens. Our brains are wired to pair things together, particularly anything that holds significance for us. A song that once was just a pleasant tune can become deeply meaningful and emotionally evocative because it happened to be playing when something memorable occurred, like the first time you kissed your partner. Likewise, alcohol and drug use can link up with reminders of their own. Beer advertisements during the Super Bowl, a certain bar or lounge where drinking used to happen, a particular street related to drug use, or vivid smells that always used to go along with drinking or using—such as cigarettes, the smell of the alcohol or drugs themselves, or the aroma of certain foods—are all examples. And when these reminders automatically pull people's attention, they can make them more prone to experience cravings and more vulnerable to relapsing.[39]

What's more, it has also been shown that people who unconsciously link drugs and alcohol with their sense of self—with their own being, as though substances are a part of their identity—are more apt to give up on an addiction treatment program sooner. Notably, it's the unconscious attitude, not the conscious one, that forecasts people's treatment time.[40] And while we're on the topic of time, let's delve into this a bit more.

Mind Your Planning

One of the most precious resources we have is also one we can't see—time. And it affects us in ways we can't always make out. For instance, the timing of our plans impacts how much personal agency we feel when we're making decisions. Even though we don't plan ahead for everything, we plan ahead for a slew of activities in our daily routine. But because we've planned them already (e.g., eating lunch at 12:30 p.m., going to the gym at 5:00 p.m., going out to dinner and a movie at 8:00 p.m.), when the time comes to actually act on these plans, we're less apt to think about the fact that we're still choosing to do them at that moment. So when we're making these choices, we feel less personal autonomy than we would if we hadn't made plans in advance.[41] On the other hand, when we act on a plan shortly after we've made it, we don't lose as much sense of personal agency. It's tremendously ironic that the decision to plan our actions a little further in advance, which you would think gives us more personal autonomy, is actually associated with feeling less choice once the time comes for us to carry our plan out! The take-home message to us all is that we need to tune in to ourselves a bit more and look at all of the choices we're making in the moment, both grand and small. For instance, if you go for an evening walk after work, rather than just doing it, pay attention to the fact that you're doing it. And if you wish to pick up on even more details during your walk, try taking in the sights, sounds, smells, and sensations that are there with you.

The Concealed Benefit of Brands

We also have ideas about ourselves that are concealed from our view, yet bear upon our performance. In the inner recesses of your mind, do you believe that your talents are set in stone? Or do you implicitly believe that your talents are the reflection of time and effort, with wiggle room to improve? If, at an unconscious level, you believe the former, the brands you use could lend you a leg up when you're trying to do your best. People who unconsciously believe their talents are set feel a higher sense of competence when they do things like take a difficult test with a pen from an elite university, or drink water from a container with the logo of a popular energy drink when they vigorously exercise. This won't help you if you implicitly believe your talents can shift, but otherwise, brands associated with high performance and success can bolster your endeavors![42]

True Grit

Another example of how unconscious ideas mold our behavior is our latent beliefs about willpower. Does willpower have a shelf life and run out, or do humans have unlimited willpower? Whatever we implicitly believe affects how much we're inclined to take a rest between finishing a demanding mental task and starting another one. Those of us who unconsciously believe that willpower is a limited commodity are more inclined to take rest breaks, whereas folks who see willpower as an ever-flowing fountain do not feel as motivated to take them.[43] In your own life, you've likely noticed diverse styles that people have of moving toward a goal. Some people can persist in their efforts for extended periods of time, whereas other folks go in spurts. Apply this to yourself. How do you generally prefer to strive toward a goal? After a strenuous effort, is it your fancy to take a break, or do you feel propelled toward the next task? Regardless of what outlook you have, these unseen, unconscious notions about how much self-control and self-discipline you believe people have on reserve exert a powerful impact on your conscious experience of feeling like you need rest or not after you complete each challenge. There's no right or wrong answer. The key is to know your own style and match your choices to what works best for you.

The Price Is Right

If someone asked you what impacts your decision to buy something, what would you say? I don't know about you, but of all the things I *wouldn't* have thought about, it's how much I personally connect to the numbers on the price tag. That's right. If we unconsciously think well of ourselves (and on the whole, people do), the actual numbers can sway our purchasing decisions without our even realizing it. For instance, we're more apt to like a product and want to buy it if the price contains numbers that we unconsciously link to ourselves. A snack with a cost that matches your birthday? Sold. A price tag with a number that begins with the same letter as your name? Nina, Ned, or Nancy is inclined to buy it if it's nine dollars and twenty cents. Not only that, we're more likely to want the item that costs more moola.[44] So the next time you're itching to buy a product, spend a little more time considering just why you want to buy it!

Give Me That Glare

Finally, let's consider how people look at us. Which would you rather confront—an angry face looking straight at you or an angry face looking away? Strikingly, new research suggests we have such a potent wish for attention that, at an unconscious level, we actually prefer a person's angry face looking head-on at us. You'd likely never imagine that you'd go for an angry person looking right at you, but if it's that versus being ignored, odds are that you would.[45] This supports folk wisdom that any attention is better than none. So if you find yourself feeling upset and acting out toward someone, or if someone is being out of line with you, you might want to consider whether a yearning for attention is playing a role.

I sincerely hope that this tour of what we shy away from within us was illuminating. As we've seen repeatedly, it can be healthful to escape the unpleasant and unwanted in our inner world. At the same time, it's also a crucial tool to deal with what fills us with unease. Regardless of whether we turn the dial up or down on what we don't want, if we can do so in a balanced way that's flexible to our needs and circumstances, then we're wielding the power of escapism beautifully. Now, we'll move on to exercises to help you cultivate some of the skills we've covered, and from there we'll move up to the next level of denial: denial at the level of ourselves.

EXERCISES

Exercise 1: Shining a New Light

We learned in this chapter that one of the ways we turn down the dial on what we don't want in our inner world is reinterpretation. Now let's try putting it into practice! Imagine that you are actually in each situation described below (e.g., your alarm for work doesn't go off). Then use a separate sheet, digital or paper, to write how you would feel in each situation (e.g., stressed, anxious, frustrated). Next, try to come up with a way to reframe each situation in a new, more upbeat light ("Well, this happens to everyone sometimes. Besides, at least I got a little more shut-eye!"). Finally, write how you feel after this new way of seeing the situation (e.g., calm, slightly amused). Notice whether you turned down the emotions you felt before the reframe. There's no right or wrong answer; just be honest with yourself!

1. Situation: You're exhausted after a long day at work, and unbeknownst to you, construction is causing gridlock traffic on your drive home. You see the cars at a standstill, snaking along the road.

   How you feel:

   Your reframe:

   How you feel now:

2. You realize that the career path you've chosen is not the right one for you. But you've spent years getting there, and now you're at a loss with what to do next.

   How you feel:

   Your reframe:

   How you feel now:

3. You enrolled in a community college course convinced that you'd ace it. Now you find you've failed your class in spite of your best efforts.

   How you feel:

   Your reframe:

   How you feel now:

4. You've been dating your partner for eight months. You're developing strong feelings for this person, and you can picture a long-term future together. Then one night, your partner breaks up with you, saying that you're just not a good fit.

   How you feel:

   Your reframe:

   How you feel now:

5. You've long believed that it's totally unacceptable to feel frightened, angry, or sad. But then, after some difficult challenges in life, you find that you're feeling all three.

   How you feel (about having these feelings):

   Your reframe:

   How you feel now:

6. You've been in recovery for the past two years. Then, after a night of binge drinking, you wake up hungover. On your voice mail is a message from your AA sponsor asking where you were last night, wanting to make sure you're OK.

   How you feel:

   Your reframe:

   How you feel now:

Exercise 2: Shining a Light on What We Shirk

On this stop of our tour, we delved into ways we sidestep what feels uncomfortable and disquieting. In this exercise, you'll have a chance to look at what you stay away from in your own life. As you do this exercise, if you feel a desire to stop, feel free to do so. That's OK! If that happens, I invite you to ask yourself why you're stopping to understand it better. Also, you might feel an uptick in upsetting feelings during this exercise. If you're willing to sit with these feelings, that's fine. If you think you're probably not, try planning some enjoyable, distracting activities that you can do afterward, such as watching a comedy, chatting with a friend, playing with a beloved pet, or going out for a walk in a beautiful space. As with the other exercises, use a separate sheet to respond.

1. How do you react when the following emotions come up for you?

   Sadness

   Surprise

   Anger

   Disgust

   Fear/anxiety

   Happiness

   Love

   Embarrassment

2. We're inclined to steer clear of some situations more than others because they bring up uncomfortable feelings. What kinds of situations or circumstances do you evade to keep unwanted feelings at arm's length?

3. We've been talking a lot about how we cope with distress. Please reflect on how you cope with physical sensations, feelings, and thoughts that you don't want. As you list the different tools you use, consider whether these tactics are helpful in the short run and the long run.

   a. My coping repertoire is:

   b. When I think about which strategies really work for me, and which ones may help in the short term but not in the long term, I'd say:

3

DENIAL AT THE LEVEL OF OURSELVES

I could deny it if I liked. I could deny anything if I liked.
—Oscar Wilde, *The Importance of Being Earnest*

In the last chapter, we toured through happenings within us that we'd rather not see. Now, on this segment of our journey, we're standing at the level of who we are: where the histories, identities, and aspirations we carry with us live. Prepare yourself to take a trip through the varied spaces where we ward off those nuggets of ourselves that we'd rather not behold. Bob's experience is a classic example.

"Wake up, Bob!" Bob's wife, Leigh, exclaims, shaking him awake. Bob jolts as he opens his eyes and takes in the sight of his wife and their bedroom, rather than the jungles of Vietnam that furnished his nightmare.

"Poor thing. You were screaming and thrashing around. Are you alright now? Would you like some water?" Leigh tenderly asks as she strokes his head.

"No, sweetheart," Bob reassures his wife, fondly covering her hand with his. "I'm OK. Just a nightmare, I guess. I don't even remember what it was about," he fibs.

As they turned out the light, Bob stews. Another Vietnam nightmare? Jesus, Bob, get over it! That was 1970. It's 2016!

Don't let the details of Bob's ordeal fool you into thinking that only veterans encounter this type of scenario. To be sure, the experience of returning home from deployment and grappling with combat nightmares is unique to veterans, but the elemental bedrock of Bob's story is a prevalent one. It's denial of a piece of ourselves, and it wears a myriad of guises:

- spurning our past
- rebuffing our identity or a part of who we are
- keeping back from a forthright look at our personal flairs and flaws
- turning down our needs and wants

THANKS FOR THE PAST, BUT YOU CAN KEEP IT

Memories: They're manna from heaven at times. Those rosewater, mental mementos of dreamy times with your sweetheart, affectionate images of a faraway time when you playfully jostled with your siblings, and a host of other fond, cheerful occasions. They gladden the heart, don't they? Yet, as Bob knows all too well, memories can torment too. A harrowing, traumatic ordeal, like a car accident, combat, robbery, or rape. The searing image of that mistake you can never take back still brings a cringe. Even seemingly delightful memories can become agonizing ones, depending on the context. Dreamy dates with your beloved suddenly jab like bayonets in the gloom of grief following his death; silly childhood doings with the family pass into melancholy after a tragedy. If these don't fit, undoubtedly you can conjure up unpleasant examples tailored to your own life.

So what do we do when the daggers of days gone by come calling? Despite the fact that memories don't literally gash us, at times they can feel so shameful or shattering that we cower at their stinging force. It's akin to keeping Pandora's box. We live in dread that the demons we locked away will engulf us if we dare lay eyes on them. What's especially inhumane is that, by and large, it's our most distressing dragons of the past, the ones we most yearn to forget, that seem so masterful at strong-arming our psyche.

If we hoist a sturdy barricade between ourselves and troubling memories, we're essentially neglecting an injury. And when we repeatedly fend off aching memories, that wound, like an unattended injury, is likely to fester.[1] Those who habitually dodge memories of trauma are more apt to struggle with depression and anxiety.[2] Alcohol and other drug use offers another means of escape, but as we talked about in the last chapter, even as it appears to work in the short run, it doesn't heal the past and only creates more troubles in the end.[3] Surprisingly, even ruminating about the past (such as gloomily thinking about upsetting memories and our reactions to them over and over again) seems to be a disguised form of avoidance. As dismal as rumination is, it can actually be an evasion tactic that shields us from thinking about very particular, distinct memories or thoughts that are even more daunting and anguishing, such as the death of a family member or partner. And then what happens? Ultimately, as with mood-altering substances, rumination works against us, getting in the way of our own healing after the loss of a loved one.[4]

No matter what we do to avoid painful memories, most of us who endure a trauma (e.g., physical or sexual assault, war) or a powerfully painful experience (e.g., bereavement, divorce, or loss of a home or a job) will face unwelcome memories of those dire moments now and then. Sadly, a lot of us will deal with these invading reminders while grappling with another albatross like depression, post-traumatic stress disorder (PTSD), or a substance use disorder.[5] This can add to the burden of the stigma associated with mental illness or addiction and prevent us from seeking the professional help we need. Fortunately, more veterans and other trauma survivors are finding the courage and support to overcome that stigma and are finding healing by bringing their buried pain into the light of day, where its power is defused.

Even when we migrate from the realm of the severely upsetting to the milder domain of feeling blue, we often still prefer to stand at arm's length from those unpleasant mental snapshots.[6] But perhaps we don't want to elude these memories entirely. Maybe we just want a little elbow room to look at them differently. If we can think back on our past from a more faraway, aerial perspective, as if we're reflecting on a third person, we're more apt to view prior hurts in a broader and more graspable way.[7] One tried-and-true way of facing an aching experience in the past is by jotting down our most profound emotions and thoughts about it. Notably, reframing our way of looking at the past as we're writing can actually help us heal.[8] In the end, whether we gravitate toward the written or spoken word, or both, it is owning these memories and expressing our feelings, rather than darting away from them, that will take away their power in our lives. We can then come to know and accept ourselves for who we are in the present rather than living in the past.

CAN WE KEEP THIS SKELETON LOCKED SOMEWHERE . . . ANYWHERE?

What if it's not our past, but a piece of who we are that we'd like to lock away? Perhaps this part of ourselves is buried in stigma and shame. Secretly, we yearn to be different than we are so we can just fit in and make folks happy. Or maybe we just feel uneasy about a part of ourselves and would rather step away from it. Alternatively, perhaps it's not a part of us that we're talking about, but a label that we simply refuse to own for ourselves. Regardless of what guise it takes, this type of denial leaves behind a palpable residue on our well-being and our lives. In this next section, we're going to roam diverse slices of our selfhood that we're prone to hold back from owning.

Shielding Ourselves and Fitting In

Have you ever been in a difficult situation when your lack of self-confidence made you want to escape and avoid facing it? Did you pick up on why you felt that way? Sometimes the reason isn't always evident. There's just a subtle, hazy feeling of being set apart or deflated. At other times, the "why" is clearer. You may believe that there is something you "should" have and lack (education, money, intelligence, good looks, a way with words, or being "normal"). Or you might feel tense when your gender, race, sexual orientation, age, or socioeconomic status, to name a few factors, stands out in a particular situation. Take Yvonne, for instance.

When Yvonne received the acceptance letter to college, she was delirious with joy. She lives in poverty, so the full scholarship she received represented her ticket in. But as she drifts into the first party of college, a cloud of inadequacy envelopes her as she sees how well-off everyone looks. Even though people cordially welcome her, she feels self-conscious and ill-suited to be there.

Now let's be straight up. Most of us want to feel satisfied with ourselves, that we're alright and A-OK. So it can be downright scary to be who we are, especially if it means facing messages that we're unacceptable in some way. It's not always easy to choose between presenting ourselves as an authentic individual who marches to the beat of their own drum and conforming to the crowd. And when our self-regard feels vulnerable, we'll mobilize our own defense like a loyal sentry. But we don't do this in a vacuum. As in Yvonne's case, context plays its part. For instance, a 2015 study reveals that how much we deny fluctuates with our culture. The less affluent a country's residents are, the more they rebuff unflattering facts about themselves (e.g., denying that they talk about other people behind their backs), seemingly to blend in alongside others.[9] When our sense of self-confidence feels like it's on thin ice, we'll alter our purchasing habits, leaning away from low-cost wares in favor of pricier items, as ritzier goods tend to elevate our self-assurance.[10]

Concealing Our Identity

Then again, there are times that we'd sooner camouflage a part of who we are that we believe blemishes us. It's not possible to cloak every aspect of ourselves, such as our race or age. But we may—whether we really have to or not—feel we need to try to conceal painful information about ourselves: our HIV status, psychological conditions we may deal with, a history of being sexually or physically assaulted, our sexual orientation, our gender identity, or whether we grapple with alcohol or other drug abuse, to name a few. Consider Carly's circumstance.

Carly has been married to Luther for the past ten years. By all appearances, she has a nearly idyllic life. She's on a skyward career path, has a bevy of friends, and has Luther by her side, a fetching, personable husband whom everybody adores. Little do they know that Luther beats her in discreet places on her body that he knows her clothes will conceal. Despite her profound wish to leave, the feelings of weakness and humiliation for marrying Luther and staying with him after all this time are too suffocating for her to say something about it and seek help.

This strategy of concealment may buy us armor against others' possible displeasure and scorn—but does it *really* help us feel better? Not really. As with Carly, who carried shame with her even though no one else knew, the mere belief that others will react with scorn if they know about whatever is being concealed is linked to lower physical health and mental well-being.[11] When we veil an identity we're ashamed of, it can actually curtail our self-control when we're relating to others, along with our mental sharpness and physical strength.[12]

Another feature of ourselves that we hide is an all-too-commonplace one: when we're in debt and are unable to keep up with our bills. For example, one study reveals that not only do some people view their mortgage troubles as a stigma in others' eyes, they personalize it and feel debased. And even as they may strive to safeguard themselves by keeping it a secret, they can also grow more socially secluded and weighed down with anguish, sorrow, and nervousness.[13]

So far we've talked about stigma on a more general level. In this next section, let's delve into some of the particular types of identities we turn away from that, more often than not, come stigma-laden.

Burying Our Mental Health

If we struggle with mental health issues and feel shame about it, we often take this on as a core part of our identity that we need to disguise, and we will even opt to languish in misery rather than seek help. Depression is a powerful example, in part because it's incredibly widespread, with roughly 20 to 55 percent of us grappling with it at some point in life. In spite of the fact that so many of us suffer, most of us will keep our suffering a secret at work, a place where we spend a sizable amount of time, and where it's been shown that only a third of people who live with depression say they would find it easy to talk with their manager about their condition.[14]

And what we see on television and in the movies can have an impact too, for better or worse. The on-screen depictions we see of people wrestling with psychological pain, mental health providers, and people in therapy hold the potential to sway our mental picture of how we see both psychologists and people who suffer. Media portrayals are also connected to how we would view ourselves if we were hurting emotionally and sought help from a therapist.[15] Sadly, shame about getting help for mental health issues predicts diminished self-esteem and lower odds of deciding to reach out for help.[16] It's been shown that military service members struggling with mental illness who have internalized the shame of public stigma and view themselves as unworthy are especially reluctant to seek therapy.[17] Fortunately, it's possible to resist buying into public stigma, and to treat others and ourselves with deeper understanding and kindness. How can we do this? One way is to comprehend the emotional problems people face as a common human struggle (rather than as an "abnormal" challenge). People who adopt this perspective are more prone to feel compassion for those who are struggling with emotional pain and to reach out for psychological help themselves if they need it.[18]

Going into Hiding with Gender

People whose gender identity differs from the gender they were assigned at birth (e.g., someone who was raised female but whose gender identity is male) must wrestle with the agonizing daily reality of living a façade if they choose to conceal who they truly are. Tragically, the consequences of being honest and living in line with their gender identity can be lethal, leading people who identify as transgender to flee for their lives from their own communities.[19]

But what of people whose gender identity matches the gender they were assigned at birth? Although they certainly have the luxury of living without the same hardships and fear, gender identity weighs upon their sense of self too. Gender carries the baggage of gender norms, the expectations of what it means to be an "appropriate" man or woman. The thing about these norms is that they're boilerplates—but we aren't. So, just as gender is a central part of many people's identity, gender norms hold the potential to, ironically, lead us to turn aside from our true, authentic self.

Vernon's situation is a fitting illustration of the potent impact of gender roles.

Vernon is a thirty-year-old engineer who loves his job. In his private life, he's an avid runner with a wide circle of friends. When he's with his guy friends, he easily goes along with their jokes about things like "crying like a girl" and the absurdity of "chick flicks." Despite his aura of confidence, internally he winces in these moments, feeling faulty and feeble because he knows that he feels strong emotions at times, cries, and actually enjoys romantic comedies. In shame, he doesn't admit this side of himself to anyone, forcing himself to manage unsettling feelings alone with a few extra drinks now and again.

No doubt you can think of plenty of examples of gendered expectations from your own experience. So what imprint do these norms leave on our lives? A big one. It turns out that guys who buy into male gender norms are less apt to seek therapy,[20] tend to neglect their health (self-care remains linked to femininity),[21] and evade what they think women like when their manhood feels in jeopardy.[22] One study shows that even mere pictures depicting traditional manhood (e.g., competing in athletics) leave men more liable to buy into flawed notions of sexual activity (e.g., "a real man who doesn't sexually satisfy a woman is a failure") and unbalanced standards for sex (e.g., "a man should be more sexually experienced than his wife"), ideas that are also linked to sexual dysfunction.[23] And belief in male gender identity norms is actually linked to a more developed capacity to end one's life, placing people who hold these views at greater risk of suicide.[24]

On the gender flip side, it's been shown that women, who have a tougher time breaking into male-dominated careers or upper levels of management, are, regrettably, less likely to ace the job interview unless they portray themselves in traditionally masculine terms, such as being self-assured, self-reliant, and focused on accomplishment. Actions such as being pleasant and caring for others are labeled as traditionally feminine, a stereotype that presses down on many women.[25] Another stereotype about women is that they are defenseless and dependent, and when women think about this stereotype, they're less likely to reach out for help. Even if women do allow themselves to ask for help, they're more liable to feel lousy about it.[26]

Deflecting Race

Like gender, our racial or ethnic identity undoubtedly bears upon how we navigate our day-to-day lives and on our well-being. Consider Greg's situation at work.

Greg is a thirty-five-year-old Asian American journalist who's just received the job of his dreams as a news anchor. During his first day, he realizes that he's the only Asian employee, which gives him the feeling of standing out in a mostly White office and doubles the self-consciousness that typically comes with any first day on the job. As he questions whether he'll be accepted, he plays down his racial background whenever possible. The next day, a coworker invites him to lunch and asks where he'd like to go. Although his favorite restaurant is right down the street, a Japanese place with excellent sushi, he steers clear from mentioning it. "Let's try that Italian place a few blocks away," he says, "I've heard the food is amazing."

Greg uses avoidance in this situation to manage how his coworker sees him, one of several strategies people use in an attempt to control others' impressions of their racial or ethnic identity at work.[27] But avoidance and denial of racial identity certainly play out more broadly in daily life. For instance, African Americans who deny giving any thought to their race even though they encounter racist experiences will typically wrestle with lower psychological well-being than people who acknowledge them.[28] What's more, our identities often mingle with each other in crucial ways. For example, African American women who buy into the notion of a "strong Black woman," a concept born from trials such as a history of slavery and racial, sexual, and economic oppression, can be more prone to handle problems in solitude. Sadly, this concept is also related to depression and distress, and less of a tendency to reach out for a helping hand.[29]

Shunning Sexual Orientation

Another vital part of identity for many of us is our sexual orientation, as Devin and Reed's story illustrates.

Reed walks into the restaurant ahead of Devin. "Table for two, please," Reed says casually, "I've got a buddy joining me, but he's a bit late." Over dinner, they exchange subtle romantic glances, with a glint of fear under the surface as they try to pretend they were just friends, not on a date. Later that night, Reed breaks the stillness as they embrace each other at Devin's apartment. "We should come out, Devin. We shouldn't be afraid of all this. Same-sex marriage is legal now," Reed sighs.

"Remember what happened to Pete last week?" Devin asks. "He got the crap beat out of him by a bunch of guys who don't care what the Supreme Court says. And my family doesn't care, either. They'd hate me forever if they knew."

Our sexual orientation dramatically impacts how we feel about ourselves and our life. People who identify as gay, lesbian, bisexual, or questioning, but who buy into the idea that a heterosexual orientation is "normal," are more apt to feel unsettled and upset in their lives. This is especially true for people who lack kinship with other sexual minorities and who tend to be hard on themselves.[30] Not only that, a study in the journal *Psychology of Men & Masculinity* suggests that men who believe they're "less than" for being gay are more prone to place the stigma and self-reproach that they feel onto their partner, which predicts dwindling devotion to their bond.[31]

Deflecting Labels

Have you ever heard the phrase "words matter"? They really do. And we don't hesitate to throw them around, either, especially labels. Picture a child hopped up on candy who just got an infinite supply of sticky notes and pens, along with instructions to label everything in sight. Say hi to your brain! It's dizzying all of the labels we use, especially considering that heaps of those labels carry pretty weighty meanings. And the labels we own versus those we turn down or outright deny bear upon how we feel. For instance, kids who endure bullying at school, but who deny the description "victim," tend to feel less emotional distress and have fewer behavior problems compared to kids who take it on.[32]

Let's think about other labels. While you were in the marrow of distress, addiction, or adversity, did you tag yourself as "weak," "broken," "crazy," or "messed up"? In solitude, did you own stigma and shame because of your gender identity, race, sexual orientation, age, socioeconomic status, or physical or mental health, to name just a few? What was it like? Probably not a big boost to your self-esteem, right? Thankfully, we have a choice about what labels we choose to hang on to and which ones we let go of. We can writhe in our own mental self-slamming, or we can look at our background, our quirks, and our history of surviving addiction, psychological pain, and other hardships in life as part of what makes us "courageous," "hardy," "singular," "human," and other more affirming labels.

THAT JUST AIN'T ME . . .

"So, tell me about yourself." We've all fielded that loaded question—on a job interview, on a first date, at a party, during group gatherings. It's a first-rate invitation to share ourselves that furnishes freedom in how we answer. Then there's another one that's more specific, and practically a given at job interviews: "What are your strengths and weaknesses?" But let's say you're talking to someone you trust (and you're not in a job interview!), or you're asking yourself this question. Would you truthfully acknowledge your foibles and strong suits, or would you bat them away like Ping-Pong balls? If you're like a lot of people, you've done both at one time or another. Like that critique of yourself that you didn't want to hear but knew was right, or those loving, kind words that pinpointed the best in you. And what about the comment that felt so off base it was out in left field, or a shining view of you that someone shared, but you couldn't bring yourself to buy? No matter whether we own or deny our gifts—or our personal struggles or shortcomings—the effect lingers.

Let's start with our talents and the glistening sides of our character. Can we turn those down? Sure we can. If you doubt that, just think about the times in your life when someone got real with you and pointed out the gifts and excellences they see in you. Did you buy all of them, or was there even one time when you thought to yourself, *Yeah . . . I just don't see myself that way!* or maybe *she doesn't really know me*? Perhaps it was a particular quality, like your knack for organization, your people savvy, your athletic aptitude, or your sense of humor. But we can brush off the good within us in a broader, all-inclusive way too, particularly if we have low self-esteem and just don't hold ourselves in an appreciative light. People with low self-esteem can even be reluctant to accept that their romantic partners think highly of them, viewing their regard as courtesy.[33]

What about the flip side, denial of the personal adversities we face in life? Addiction is a good example: Denial of a drinking problem is acknowledged to be one of the key factors in why alcoholics won't seek help.[34] Arguably, people deny a problem with alcohol and other drugs for many reasons. One reason we covered in the last chapter is evasion of the distressing feelings that lead them to use in the first place. Another one that's relevant here is a reluctance to admit that they can't control their alcohol or drug use, especially if they see other folks who seem able to do so. Every time I hear the question "Why can't I drink like a 'normal' person?" I think of a lion's mouth. For alcoholics, drinking is like sticking their heads in a lion's mouth. If they get bitten, that doesn't make them weak, yet they, and sometimes even their friends and family, buy into the notion that it does. An alcoholic's struggle to stop drinking despite the harmful consequences attests to the power of their addiction, not their frailty.

In the realm of a different addictive substance, roughly half of people who smoke cigarettes now and again reject the idea that they're smokers. Although they smoke less than people who acknowledge that they're smokers, unfortunately, they're also less prone to try to quit.[35] Of course, these examples reflect how the choice to turn away from challenges we're facing can disserve us. Yet they only tell one side of the tale. At times, denial of the stumbling blocks we face lends us a vital leg up and the will to stick things out. Athletes are a sterling example. A 2015 study showed that over 81 percent of collegiate-level baseball players took their top batting achievement as the gauge of their athletic prowess. Were they on target? Eh, not so much. It turns out that their lowest showing at bat was the more accurate barometer of their performance, and the more bottom-rung athletes tended to show this bias most. On the whole, even as we can stymie ourselves from growing from our mistakes and improving our abilities if we self-delude too much, a heaping spoonful of self-enhancing denial to embellish our view of our abilities and keep us bound and determined to meet our goals is just the ticket at times![36]

MY NEEDS AND WANTS? HUH?

In the last two sections, we had a look at how we can walk away from elements of our identity and wave away a frank look at our flaws and strong suits. But we can also deny our needs and wants, putting ourselves on the back burner for something else we want, or for something else we think we "should" do—what I like to call "The Tyranny of the Shoulds."

Turning Down the Dial on Our Needs and Wants: The Downside

To be sure, it's beneficial for us to tell ourselves what we "should" do, particularly when it's good for us. Take speeding, for instance. Have you ever been driving along the road and felt hemmed in from going as fast as you really wanted? Yet, in spite of your momentary identification with a corralled racehorse, you restrained yourself and did what you knew you should do. Or perhaps, as your vacation drew to a close, you weren't exactly itching to go back. Yet you realized that people were counting on you, and so, even as it felt like swimming in molasses to return, you went because it felt like the right thing to do. A healthy dollop of "should" can be a good thing.

On the other hand, if we take it too far, we risk living a life of disregarding ourselves and denying those authentic needs and earnest wants at the core of who we are, which can arguably sap our development, thriving, and quality of life. It hollows us out. This dynamic of self-denial plays out against the backdrop of our lives, and it pops up early on. For instance, even though most parents will good-naturedly heap over-the-top praise on children with low self-esteem to uplift their self-regard, they sadly may end up sabotaging that very aim. Instead, their accolades can inadvertently tell children they have Herculean benchmarks to meet. Ironically, this ups the odds that they'll run from challenges to guard themselves against falling short, rather than aspire to meet them.[37]

Even farther along the path of life in adulthood, we can be more apt to aim for others' passions than our own in situations when we feel the following:[38]

- hindered from pursuing what we innately relish and care about, feeling the tug of reasons less dear to our hearts instead, like making money, boosting our self-esteem, evading guilt or stigma, or pleasing others
- more disconnected and cut off from the people in our lives
- less capable, qualified, or skillful

A wrinkle in our ability to follow our needs and wants is that a vital layer of our needs and wants is missing from our view, ordinarily concealed in the world of our unconscious. Even if we think we know what we want, our unconscious wishes sit in the dark, left out of the equation of our conscious choices. It's kind of like trying to eat a whole cake and only being able to taste the frosting. If you had several cakes in front of you and were trying to select the best one, how would you know if you only sampled the top part? You're more liable to pick a cake that doesn't suit your palate. Likewise, imagine someone telling you that you'd have to go through life making decisions armed with a portion of the knowledge of what you truthfully want and need. In essence, that's our lot, only without someone at the starting gate to warn us first. This wedge between what we think we want (the icing) and what we truly want (the full cake) makes us more prone to toil toward aspirations that don't fulfill or gratify us. Take Geraldo's situation.

As he was growing up, Geraldo's middle-class, hardworking parents dreamed that he'd have an even better lot in life than they did, and they urged him to go into law, knowing he could pull it off. He knew he could too, feeling especially drawn toward corporate law, specializing in mergers and acquisitions. He walked into his career with a sense of elation, taking his excitement as a sign that he must be doing the right thing.

As the long work hours and years float by, Geraldo fulfills his dream of living a wealthy lifestyle, yet he finds no joy in it all. He rationalizes his position, telling himself that no one actually likes their job, that the road toward easy street is neither easy nor enjoyable. He keeps up that story until the depression and drinking start. With the help of some soul searching in therapy, he realizes that the thrill of corporate law came from pleasing his parents and knowing that he attained their standard of success—making a lot of money. Courageously, he walks away from his firm and opens up a flower shop, a pipe dream he'd told himself he could indulge in when he retired. And for the first time in his life, he is walking on air.

Fortunately, we don't necessarily have to resign ourselves to a life of frosting. According to Dr. Kenneth Sheldon, a psychological researcher at the University of Missouri–Columbia and an expert in goals and well-being, it's possible to connect more with who we are—our stable character traits, passions, and principles. He holds out a number of ways to bolster our ability to aim for authentic, healthful wants and needs in life.[39]

- *Foster freedom of expression and choice.* Arguably, this can apply across all areas of our lives—to our jobs where employees are given more voice, in a romantic relationship, with family, in our daily routine, or in our communities. Remember how we touched upon the challenge of being true to ourselves when we're feeling hemmed in by other factors like guilt, self-esteem, stigma, people pleasing, money, or feeling unskilled or detached from people? Arguably, where we can find or create spaces in life with more freedom to choose, and where we feel more confident and connected, we'll be more able to strive for what we sincerely want.
- *Try mindfulness meditation.* It's a highly effective practice of nonjudgmentally observing bodily sensations (e.g., muscle tension, breathing rate), thoughts, and feelings that arise, as well as what we notice around us in our life. There are workbooks and classes available that you can try. You'll find some options at the end of this book in the Resources section.
- *Paint a picture of your feelings.* When you think about the menu of options as you're making a choice, try conjuring up how you would likely feel if you made each one.
- *Spot your blind spots.* At the same time, we're not the greatest fortune tellers when it comes to knowing how we'll feel, so you might want to try this idea before you try the one above. Keep in mind specific ways you're apt to run aground when you try to predict how you'll feel in a particular situation. We humans make sundry errors. At times, we unintentionally exaggerate our guess

of how we'd feel in certain situations, like how upset we'd be if we didn't get that promotion. Another error we make is zooming in on how only one thing (e.g., the promotion) is likely to affect our feelings while forgetting about the many other influences in our life (our romantic partner, friends, hobbies, health, etc.). Another notable miscalculation is that we're prone to underestimate our ability to build meaning around stressful life events and to heal.[40]

- *Use people—in a good way.* Isn't it amazing how your closest, most worthwhile supporters seem to know what's best for you, even more than you do at times? Draw on them as a resource and ask what they recommend for you.
- *Plug in to your principles.* Do you know what your most gratifying, deep-seated values are? Not only do they reflect your authentic needs and wishes, but they're also linked to greater contentment in life, so try listening to them. Do you wish to build closer relationships, help other people, cultivate greater spirituality, or nurture self-growth? Whatever values you cherish, consider reflecting on their significance in your life.[41]

Not only is it possible to make choices that are more in line with our true, genuine needs and wants, we reap the benefits from doing so. When we're aiming for a goal because we sincerely want it, those decoys that can lure us astray become less seductive, like the itch to nosh on that hot fudge sundae, bag that workout, pick up that cigarette, or toss back that drink.[42] We're also more liable to actually stick to our guns when we're aiming for goals that map to what we truly want,[43] and we're more likely to reach them too.[44] What's more, people who honor their need for relaxation and fun have more peace of mind.[45]

Turning Down the Dial on Our Needs and Wants: The Upside

OK, before this starts to sound like a bash session on setting aside our needs and wants, let's step back and take in the panoramic view. We don't always turn away from needs and wants to serve a "should" or a desire that isn't really in our best interest (such as to win people's approval). Oftentimes, we find ourselves putting one need or want on ice in the name of a larger one, and that capacity to delay gratification and prioritize higher, long-term needs and wants brings noteworthy perks.[46] Consider Ellen's story.

> *For years, Ellen has been telling herself that she's going to take better care of her health, and she's long dreamed of finishing a competitive running event. When she decides to enter a 10K run, she tells herself,* you just have to do it, Ellen. If you enter, you'll actually train for it. *In the lead-up to the race, she joins a running club for support and lets the sacrifices begin. Gone are those mellow, contented weeknight evenings snuggled up on the couch, binge-watching the latest hot cable TV series. Sweat, discomfort, muscle soreness, and occasional setbacks take their place. Temptations to quit loom, so she sticks inspirational quotes to the fridge to inspire her to see it through. She turns down dining out with her friends on evenings when she has club practices. Although she misses these rewarding, comfortable treats in her life, she knows she won't reach her goal if she only trains sporadically. The day of the race, as she crosses the finish line feeling empowered, with more muscle tone, elevated energy, and five pounds lighter, the delay of gratification is worth it all.*

Ellen's tale is just one example of how waving goodbye to certain needs and wants to advance larger ones can serve us faithfully. There are plenty of others:

- putting more money into retirement

- saying no to some fun nights out and yes to studying for that exam that will open doors to a personally rewarding career if you do well
- making loving sacrifices to help your romantic partner and strengthen your bond, such as taking on a chore you dislike to spare your sweetheart from having to do it
- working toward your long-term health by replacing that tasty afternoon candy bar with an apple to boost your fruit and vegetable intake

So our knack in turning down the dial on what we want or need in the here and now with a larger end goal in mind is an exceedingly handy tool to possess. How do we harness it?

- *Grow your gratitude garden.* If you're trying to show more fiscal restraint, consider bringing thankfulness for what you have on board to help. We're more liable to make hasty financial choices when we feel distressed and low-spirited. On the other hand, gratitude has the opposite impact, leading us to show more self-control and moderation when we're making monetary decisions.[47]
- *Hatch a plan for how you'll resist traps.* Oftentimes, when we're aiming for a goal that matches our true self, that gentle pause to take a broader view and curiously ask what we're doing and the reasons why offers just what the doctor ordered. It centers us on our innermost needs and wants, and makes us resistant to the temptations of less intrinsic goals such as money, prestige, taste, or avoidance of uncomfortable feelings. But what about when we're tense and under pressure? Ironically, in those circumstances, it's actually the broader view that bites us in the rear, leaving us more apt to rationalize giving into temptation. Thankfully, we can arm ourselves

with a plan for what specific step we'll take if we encounter a tantalizing booby trap. For instance, we might tell ourselves something like "if anyone offers me a piece of cake, I'll say, 'no, thank you,'" or "if I see drugs at the party, I'll turn around and leave, then call a taxi to pick me up."[48]

- *See yourself as a doer.* It's one thing to say you enjoy cycling and another to say you're a cyclist. Folks who see what they do as a part of who they are tend to follow through and reach their aims. Of course, this strategy has its limitations. Labels such as "drinker," "heroin user," "smoker," "cheater," or "liar," are unlikely to serve anyone well.[49]

We're back to the value of balancing how we turn down the dial. Like a double-edged sword, denial can cut our capacity to flourish out from under us, or it can defend us as we climb toward superior, long-term aspirations. In the exercises that follow, we'll apply some of the lessons we've learned, and then in the next chapter, we'll look at the role denial plays in our relationships.

EXERCISES

Exercise 1: Knowing and Building Up Our True Self

On this leg of our tour, we delved into the manifold ways we shun elements of ourselves, from our identity, gifts, and personal imperfections to our wants and needs. In this exercise, you'll have an opportunity to heighten your realization of how you deny assorted pieces of yourself and to take a less critical, more compassionate second look at who you are. The goal in this exercise is not to invalidate or force a change in how you see yourself. Consider it an open door to the first step of taking stock of yourself and possibly questioning long-held assumptions. You'll want a separate sheet, digital or paper, for this exercise.

1. If you were to honestly describe the essence of what makes you who you are—your identity—what would you say?

2. Which parts of yourself do you respect?

3. Which parts of yourself feel stigmatized, feel shameful, or drain your self-respect?

4. What are your personal gifts (talents, positive characteristics, abilities, etc.)? Think both about gifts that you notice in yourself, and those that others have told you they see in you.

5. What are your own shortcomings? Make two lists: Are there any that you accept, acknowledge, and live with? What about ones that are challenging to accept?

6. Imagine that you could talk to your innermost, authentic, true self. What would this self say to you about your genuine wants and needs, and the life you're currently living versus the life you really want?

7. Imagine that you're talking to a compassionate, caring, forgiving friend who wants the very best for you in life. What would that friend say to you about (a) who you are as a person, (b) your talents and flaws, and (c) the best way to live your life?

Exercise 2: Stepping Toward the Real Me

In the previous exercise, you took stock of how you see yourself and stacked up your present life against the life your true self desires. In this exercise, you'll have a chance to step toward who you are and what you deeply want. You'll want a separate sheet to write down your answers.

1. Please list specific steps you could take that would help you to live in keeping with who you truly are and what you deeply want.

2. Now, choose one of these to actually try out in your own life.

3. After you tried it out, write down what happened: What did you feel? How did people respond? How, if at all, did it change how you feel about yourself and your life?

4. Are there any other possible steps that you'd like to take in your life next? Which one(s) and why?

4

DENIAL AT THE LEVEL OF OUR RELATIONSHIPS

Had I been in love, I could not have been more wretchedly blind. But vanity, not love, has been my folly.

—Jane Austen, *Pride and Prejudice*

At this stop on our tour of the lush and sometimes thorny landscape of relationships, you'll notice themes of previous stops. And, just as we saw on earlier stops, turning down the dial on what we don't want in relationships is a mixed bag. It can open doors for us, and it can lead us astray. Just so, we'll explore ways to make turning down the dial work for you and how to make changes when it works against you. Let's start with Milo and Trisha as an example of the latter.

Milo's words evaporate into a void of silence until his wife, Trisha, awkwardly laughs. "Oh, don't mind my husband, folks. He's just not himself today, are you, Milo?" Milo holds up his hands, embarrassment quietly choking him as he halfheartedly chuckles, "Guilty as charged!" His laughter masks hurt feelings that Trisha cut him down to size in public. On the way home, he ponders whether to tell her how he feels. What's the point? She'll just make fun of me, and then I'll feel even worse. Forget it. *Meanwhile, Trisha, not realizing she said anything harmful, notices that Milo seemed ruffled, but hesitates to say anything.*

> If something is getting at him, maybe he doesn't want to talk about it at all, or he just wants to wait until he's ready. Why can't I just say, "I love you, Milo, and I'm here for you"? But then he'll just make fun of me for being hokey. Forget it.

Milo and Trisha's story plays out every day in relationships. Picture it: the topics put off, the emotions tuned out, barriers against being open, not wanting to face how we may play a role in unpleasant moments, uncertainty about whether to end a relationship that isn't working, and the narratives we weave about our partner. They all make up part of the landscape of denial at the level of our romantic relationships. Much as we'd like to deny it, there's no getting around this plain truth: Relationships are scary! It's not that they're necessarily unnerving all of the time, or even most of the time. What I mean is that, at minimum, they have the power to shake us up at times. And what times are those? Well, that depends. Some people might tell you it's the act of revealing themselves and risking judgment, whereas for others it could be allowing themselves to be hurt by deeply loving and depending on someone. Undoubtedly, you can call up sources of fears that you have encountered in your relationships.

Regardless of what you find intimidating in a relationship, there's probably a common theme underneath: vulnerability. Relationships typically involve immense vulnerability as we open ourselves up and let someone in. We're like onions with layers that peel back, revealing inner ones, only our layers never end. I don't think it's unusual for people to think they'll reach a point where they'll know all about their partner, as if there's a specific destination that will gift them with unlimited insight into their beloved's past, heart, and mind. Let me correct that right now: No matter how well you think you know your partner, you will never, ever (and I mean never, ever) discover all there is to know. Your partner is an infinite onion, and so are you. As a psychologist, I know all too well that people, including those in longstanding relationships, can confine pieces of themselves in the recesses of their heart, fearful of sharing them with their partner or spouse. So, no matter whether you've been dating a few weeks or have been married for fifty years, there is always vulnerability. And thank goodness for that! Where there is vulnerability, there are windows to take risks, and where there is risk-taking, there is room to deepen a relationship—if we're paying attention. Yet most of us at one time or another turn away from vulnerability, preferring to be safeguarded than to be a sitting duck. So, on the ground floor of this tour, we're going to shine a light on ways we try to shield ourselves from vulnerability and how our efforts often wind up taking a chunk out of us instead.

STOP, DROP, AND HIDE

Our earliest relationships, especially the ones we had with our parents or other caregivers, serve as a sort of relationship training ground for us. From the soil of these early experiences, we develop a set of expectations for relationships that we carry with us and continue to develop in our romantic life. These expectations include what we believe we deserve in relationships, as well as how we think romantic partners will probably treat us. Understandably, they affect how we allow ourselves to bond with a romantic partner. For instance, if we believe we're worthy of love and trust, that we can count on our partner, then we have a more solid foundation on which to build a thriving, loving relationship. If either of these pieces is missing, then we're on less secure ground to form a close attachment with our partner. This insecurity can take more than one form. Perhaps we deeply crave connection, yet struggle to see ourselves as good enough to be loved, so we fearfully dread rejection and anxiously anticipate getting dumped. On the other hand, maybe we dismissively shun closeness, a wedge of indifference protectively shielding us, because we just don't believe that we can depend on anyone. Regardless of what our insecure foundation looks like, it affects how we see our partner, how we feel about ourselves, and how we attempt to guard ourselves from vulnerability.[1] Let's look at some examples.

People with a more dismissive style in their relationships are liable to falsely read more unpleasant emotion in their partner than their partner actually feels, which only adds more fuel to their tendency to fend off closeness.[2] Consider Kyle's situation.

Kyle receives a phone call from his wife, Jenna, as he logs a late night at work to meet a tight deadline. "Hi, honey," she says with concern in her voice. "Are you alright? I was worried about you."

"Why were you worried?" Kyle asks warily.

Jenna falters. "Well, you're just usually home by now and I didn't hear from you, so I got a little concerned and was hoping everything was OK."

Kyle moans, "Jenna, do you really have to start into me now? I've had a long day, and the last things I need are your hysterics and that guilt trip you're always trying to pull. I have to go now."

At home, Jenna stands with the dead phone in her hand, bewildered—and hurt.

Another example is people who frequently feel anxious as they emotionally bond with their partner, the possibility of rejection looming overhead. When their partner criticizes them, this stokes fear that their partner will leave the relationship, and they're liable to respond by amplifying how much emotional pain they express, most likely to try to arouse guilt in their partner. If this tactic works, the irony is that even though these guilty feelings soothe their own abandonment fears, the price is their partner's own diminished happiness.[3] Insecure bonding ultimately works against us in many ways: Not only is it linked with dwindling relationship happiness,[4] it also predicts diminished sexual enjoyment among women,[5] as well as greater emotional stress and physical health troubles.[6]

OK, let's stop and normalize all this. If you think you have an insecure style of bonding, it does not mean you're abnormal or "messed up." It just means that you have a set of relationship expectations that don't give you the most solid ground for a deep, trusting connection. Depending on the kind of upbringing you had, your preferred style of bonding with a romantic partner could reflect a natural response to cope with the cards life dealt you. Let's say that your caretakers were emotionally unavailable or inconsistent in their caretaking or support. It would have been adaptive for you to learn that you couldn't depend on them. Why suffer the pain of continuing to pine for parents who won't respond? So you adjust to the realities of your environment by, let's say, shunning closeness. The problem comes later, when a partner wants emotional connection, and you're holding on to the same wary style. Then what worked for you yesterday works against you today.

Thankfully, this approach isn't set in stone. For instance, people who dismiss emotional intimacy are likely to steer clear even more when their partner gives them an average level of support. But, if they're in an excellent intimate relationship[7] and receive a great deal of care and support, they're apt to turn back, moving in closer to their partner.[8] Moreover, in relationships, each partner's emotional security shifts over time in response to the other person's.[9] In other words, our style of bonding *can* change.

And in virtually all romantic relationships, there are moments of anxiety and fear. It's human. It's also understandable that we try to ignore or cover up our vulnerability, and we all have ways of doing that. The downside is that a number of them bite us in the rear. As we saw on previous stops of our tour, the harder we work to fend off something, the worse it gets. It reminds me of a golf swing—the harder you try to hit the ball into next year, the more likely it is that it *will not* happen. Trust me. Those of you who play golf know the madness I'm talking about! If you've never tried to hit a golf ball, I highly recommend it. It's a magnificent metaphor for life and for how evading vulnerability in relationships often takes us and our partner precisely where we don't want to go. Let's turn to some of these tactics.

Scouting for Security

Just as it's scary to be emotionally exposed to getting hurt, it's natural to crave signals from our partner that they love us and want to remain by our side. We may even get up the courage to ask them for reassurance, inquiring how our partner feels about us and the relationship. And as much as it's healthy to ask for what we need, if we ask for too much reassurance, our partner is more likely to create distance from us, giving us the very opposite of the closeness we seek.[10]

Circumventing a Clash

Conflict is human and inevitable at times. After all, we're talking about two unique people with their own needs and ideas, right? It's not the presence of conflict itself that gets us into hot water but how we handle it. Yet some of us swerve away from conflict as far and as speedily as we can. Sadly, the trouble is that then we're more likely to respond to later conflict with heightened reactions, especially when our partner relates to us in an antagonistic, blaming, or bossy way. And the result is even more strife with our partner, the very thing we tried to elude.[11]

Keeping a Zipped Lip

Ever heard the saying "silence is golden"? Undoubtedly, it's a nugget of astute wisdom, but sometimes, silence is more like rust than gold. Let's take Eugenie's situation.

> *Eugenie is stewing because her partner, Dolly, canceled their date to stay late at the office. Despite Dolly's efforts to call Eugenie from her office, Eugenie lets the calls go to voice mail, repeatedly. When Eugenie eventually answers the phone, the words come icily. "It's fine, Dolly. Look, I have to go. I'll see you later."*

As Eugenie illustrates, silence can actually be thunderous. And, like the lightning that precedes thunder, it can be destructive too, even though, on the face of it, silence can seem easier than actually coming out and saying what's wrong. For instance, when we brood over something that happened with our partner and keep quiet, giving the cold shoulder instead, not only does it tear down the relationship, but it also leaves us ripe for emotional burnout.[12] But it's not solely resentful silence that can eat away at connection. Research has shown a strong link between unspoken worries and anxiety, and reduced closeness and fulfillment in relationships.[13]

Concealing the Tender Spot

When we share how much we care about someone, we're going out on a limb and allowing ourselves to be vulnerable. Some folks hide the true measure of their fondness, trying to "play it cool." Or they hold back, fearful that the one they care for will brush them off or hurt their feelings. Still others hold off on showing their affection as a way of putting their partner to the test.

Now, at times, masking loving feelings can be beneficial or at least pretty harmless. A fitting example is if a person has a crush on someone at their workplace but isn't yet sure whether it feels appropriate to express it.[14] Then it can make good sense to wait and assess the situation. But, by and large, clammed-up tenderness is highly unlikely to bring you and your partner closer.[15]

Flying Solo

Sure, it feels great to know that we have what it takes to tackle demanding challenges and reach for our aspirations. But does this mean that we have to go it alone, without any help from our partner? At times, apparently, we think that's true. One study revealed that the tougher the challenges we take on, the less inclined we are to look for our partner's help. To a certain degree, we do this to protect ourselves from feeling less capable and effective, but we pay with less enjoyment in the relationship in the long run.[16] Not worth it.

Defensively Denying

As the saying goes, "to err is human." Nevertheless, it can be tough to own up to missteps on occasion, can't it? Phrases like "I goofed" or "I'm sorry" burrow inside us, refusing to come out into the open. So not only is it human to err, it's natural to feel defensive at times. Maybe it's simply too emotionally taxing to admit to ourselves that we were wrong, so we don't fess up. Or perhaps we're shielding ourselves from our partner, whom we believe will jump down our throat. No matter why we defend ourselves, one way we do it is to defensively deny, which involves rebuffing the idea that there's an issue that needs to be addressed, fending off our own accountability or trying to justify our actions. Take Greta's situation.

> *When Greta's husband, Trey, expresses his hurt that she yelled at him, she counters with, "Well, maybe if you helped me more around here, I wouldn't get so upset!" Here, she's evading responsibility for yelling at Trey and then rationalizing her actions. Perhaps this will safeguard Greta's ego, but it won't serve her marriage. If anything, it forecasts even more friction, and ultimately a less connected couple.*[17]

Safeguarding with Our Bodies

In addition to our words, or the absence of them, we can use our bodies to try to protect ourselves from feeling too exposed. Regrettably, this also tends to shuttle us in the wrong direction. For instance, people who feel highly nervous when they're in social situations are more likely to look away from others. Although the aim of this strategy is to evade anxiety, it actually heightens it.[18] Another self-defeating form of body language is when we cross our arms. Believe it or not, the act of crossing our arms causes us to feel more defensive and self-conscious. To be sure, we cross our arms for multiple reasons, including, in all likelihood, to cushion ourselves from vulnerability, but no matter why we do it, it can lead down the same road toward being more on guard.[19]

Flashing Our Trappings

We don't just stop at trying to use our bodies to arm us against vulnerability. We use material items too. Research reveals that whereas men are more likely to showcase fancy belongings to interest potential mates, women are more likely to do it to hold on to their mates, displaying pricey possessions to tell other women that their partner values them and is off-limits. It's as if to say "He's nutty about me, so don't even bother!" Even though this tactic does seem to work at throwing cold water on the competition,[20] it's a pretty expensive way of guarding against our partner leaving us behind.

Warding Off with Alcohol

Alcohol is another tool we can use to dodge vulnerability in a relationship. And, as we know all too well from earlier parts of our tour, this liquid form of self-protection can haunt us. Alcohol use to self-medicate against relationship difficulties is linked with problems in the relationship related to drinking, such as arguments and rude comments.[21] Additionally, men who rely on romantic relationships for their self-esteem are more liable to reach for the bottle in the face of troubles with their partner. Sadly, this foretells only more alcohol misuse.[22] What's more, women who face friction in their relationships are more likely to drink to manage feelings of distress and sadness. This predicts heightened troubles with alcohol, such as losing sight of obligations, drinking in dangerous conditions, or forgetting what happened when they were drinking. Not only that, it can set off a harmful chain of events as their partner follows along, elevating their own drinking and alcohol misuse in sync. But in the end, no matter why a couple drinks, couples often parrot each other's alcohol use, such that when one person escalates their drinking, the other does too.[23] This is a significant problem when we think about the health of each partner and their relationship; for instance, couples who both drink excessively are more at risk of ending their relationship than are couples who both drink a little.[24]

If there's one take-home message from this segment of our stop, it's this: Even though it can be understandably frightening to leap out and take a chance, leaving ourselves exposed and vulnerable to hurt, sometimes it's our own self-protective strategies that wound us more in the end. But putting up the barrier against vulnerability takes more than one form. Sometimes we're not trying to safeguard ourselves from being hurt but from admitting that the relationship we're in just isn't working.

GINGERLY SIDESTEPPING THE BRASS TACKS OF ROMANCE

There you are, in a relationship that's not working, but rather than acknowledge this, you perform elaborate mental acrobatics to evade that reality. I'm betting that you've either faced Waylon's situation yourself, or you know folks who have.

> *"I don't get it," Waylon sighs as he confides to his best friend, José. "Candace is such a great person, and we could be so good together. If she would only stretch herself and be a little more adventurous in life. You know, stop wasting away in that nine-to-five job with no promotion in sight. Go back to school. Pick up some new hobbies."*
>
> *"Waylon," José asks thoughtfully, "have you ever thought that maybe you're trying to force things, and Candace just isn't 'The One'?"*
>
> *"No, I don't think so," Waylon says. "She's perfect, except for those parts."*

Waylon's situation is all too commonplace. I've walked alongside people as they grappled with this. It can be beyond gut-wrenching to admit that a relationship isn't right, and at times the temptation to turn a blind eye is simply irresistible.

But let's back up to dating, before commitment, because it can even begin there. If someone who you didn't feel was right for you asked you on a date, what are the odds you'd decline? They may not be as high as you'd think. We can puff up these odds, thinking that we'd turn down a dating offer more often than we truly would. Why would we go on a date with someone when we're already noticing stop signs? Part of our motive can be to spare that person's feelings. So even at the starting gate, we may shy away from admitting that someone isn't a match.[25]

And, of course, once people are in a committed relationship, they're even more reluctant to let go and leave, which is entirely understandable. The deeper the roots of a tree, the more grueling, difficult, and painful it is to uproot. Maybe there's guilt or, as with Waylon, wishful thinking. Or perhaps people see blocks to leaving that keep them in, regardless of whether they're devoted to their partner or not. Examples of such barriers include a home, shared finances, children, the sense that others would disapprove of leaving or that it would be wrong to leave, as well as the feeling of being powerless to walk away despite wanting to do just that. In some circumstances, these barriers can be quite constructive, serving as a speed bump of sorts to help a couple stay the course rather than leave on a whim if their happiness dips for a period of time. On the other hand, they can also be detrimental, serving as fasteners that keep people in fundamentally dissatisfying, unhealthy, or abusive relationships.[26]

It can be deeply distressing to linger in a lousy relationship. And it can also ache to hover in a holding pattern, uncertain of whether to keep trying to make the relationship work or to leave. If you're grappling with this kind of ambivalent situation, I genuinely wish I could wipe your torment away. Sadly, I can't. But what I can do is hold out the small comfort that, in all probability, no matter what you decide, it won't be as agonizing as where you are right now. The anxiety-driven, stormy confusion of the unknown is the worst. So keep in mind that no matter what you do, your life and the chance to make it better await you. This is even true if you move on, as doubtful as that may seem at first. In fact, according to a 2014 study of women, divorce predicted an improvement in their mood and greater contentedness with life when they had been in a miserable marriage before. And irrespective of whether their marriage was awful or not, women who wound up with another romantic partner within three years of divorce were also more likely to feel happier.[27]

While we're on the topic of moving on, a number of people, including some relationship experts, tend to think that rebound relationships are detrimental, a destructive form of turning down the dial. They see them as risking an excessively quick move into a frivolous fling, a half-baked attempt to avoid the distress of the breakup. But is this actually true? Well, first, let's strip away the questionable assumption that a rebound relationship is naturally brief, without depth, and empty, and just ask whether it's a bad idea to spring into a new relationship not long after an old one ends. The answer is, in fact, no. If anything, it might even be the opposite. There's a link between how quickly people form a new relationship after breaking up and how happy, self-assured, and attractive they feel. So does this mean that the answer is to just rush out and start any new relationship as soon as possible? No, but it does suggest that if you find a relationship where there's the potential for love after another relationship ends, don't assume that you're leaping into an unhealthy form of denial and dooming the relationship.[28] Love whom you want, when you're ready.

SHUTTING OUR EYES TO OUR ROLE

Let's delve into another crucial way we turn down the dial. We fixate on our partner and ignore our own role in the relationship dynamics at play. I hear this in my work as a therapist, not to mention in everyday life, *a lot*. The partner is the problem, and if only the partner would change, the problem would vanish. Consider Lake and Porter.

> *Porter has been more physically distant, and it cuts Lake to the quick. "I try to cuddle with him, seduce him. Hell, I'll even settle for a hug at this point. And it's no, no, no. If he doesn't stop this, I'm leaving," Lake tells his friend Virgil.*
>
> *"Well, Lake," Virgil says, "I hate to say this, but maybe it has to do with how harshly you talk to him sometimes."*
>
> *"I'm just honest," Lake protests, "and if he can't handle that, that's his issue."*

Ultimately, Lake's approach is self-defeating. He's focusing on what he can't control—Porter—and he's neglecting the one thing he can control—himself. We're unlikely to get anywhere if we take on this mind-set, blaming our partner for relationship problems or for how they "make" us feel while neglecting our own behavior and responsibility for our feelings. So, on this next leg of our stop, we're going to look at how we turn down the dial on owning our part in the relationship and how we can play a powerful role in elevating our bond.

Tucked-Away Zingers

We humans have a knack for being able to catch the unkind words that pass our partner's lips while missing our own. A 2015 study revealed that when it comes to identifying which comments are distressing their partner, even happy couples see eye to eye only 20 percent of the time. And if you, like many people, assume that men flick off hurtful words more than women do, or that they just aren't as impacted by relationship dynamics, think again. The same study also showed that the unhappier men are in their relationship, the more hurtful words they pick up on.[29]

More Can Be Less

"Otto," Ivy sighed, "honestly, how are you ever going to get your poems published if you keep screwing off with that silly Mahjong app?" Whether you've been on the giving or receiving end, an exchange like this probably sounds familiar. On occasion, people chide their partners for giving in to distracting temptations rather than working toward their goals. The ever-so-tempting solution, it seems, is to nag. But, like the golf swing we talked about, a softer touch accomplishes more than a harder one. When we're happier in our relationship, we're actually inclined to knuckle down more to reach our goals.[30] So, rather than nagging, try fostering more joyful moments of connection with your partner and see what happens. Of course, there's no guarantee that this will be successful, but it's probably better than pestering.

Swamped by Our Own Willpower

Ah, it's just so easy to forget that a relationship is a living system and that our actions can influence how our partner sees us and treats us. One domain where this applies is how much willpower we possess to take care of what needs to get done in life. When folks are especially self-disciplined, their partner is liable to ask them to do more, operating under the belief that these added tasks are a cakewalk for them because, well, everything else seems to be. The hitch is that these people then feel more taxed, not to mention less gratified in the relationship. Arguably, this is a breeding ground for resentment: People wonder why their partner would ask so much of them. If you're in this boat, try giving your partner the benefit of the doubt that there's no ill intent behind these requests. Instead, consider setting limits and admitting to yourself and others that you can't do it all.[31]

Unplugged Because We're Plugged In

Nowadays, technology is just about everywhere—TVs, computers, tablets, and smartphones, not to mention kitchen appliances and cars that tell us what to do and where to go. Even though they're undoubtedly handy, they have the capacity to meddle in human relationships. And we're not even talking about technology addiction here, just regular use. Sure, it may not seem like those casual pauses to text, email, or catch the news have the power to monkey with a couple's bliss, but it's been shown that friction over technology use predicts lowered relationship happiness for women.[32] So, if you're arguing about your app use and are feeling more disconnected from your partner, try disconnecting from your gadgets instead.

Losing Sight of Your Place at the Party

Sure, we can overlook our role in fueling conflict, but we can pass over our ability to feed relationship joy too. When we grab the reins and do our part to be an upbeat, cheerful presence in our partner's life, it's a win for us, our partner, and our relationship. For instance, people are inclined to spend more time with individuals when they're in good spirits around them.[33] This doesn't mean you should put on a mask and hide those less-than-cheerful feelings and moments from your mate. It just means nurturing positivity within yourself and considering how you can brighten your partner's life. One powerful way you can do this is by sharing the positive highlights of your day with your partner, and being responsive and attentive when your partner shares too. This simple strategy is so potent that it predicts a deeper sense of closeness for couples, even when they're facing alarming adversity; for example, one study showed this was true for women with breast cancer.[34] There are other ways to boost a relationship's well-being too. Humor, love, sexuality, and lively and novel activities are related to relationship enthusiasm and happiness.[35] More specifically, couples who pursue interests and hobbies that are challenging yet within the scope of their abilities experience a boost in relationship enjoyment afterward.[36] But regardless of what ventures they take on, a key point is that both members of the couple need to feel motivated to pursue an interest together to get the relationship-boosting effect.[37]

To recap, we've looked at how we try to cocoon ourselves from vulnerability and from the aching dilemma of whether to remain in a relationship when we're not sure it's right. Then we explored the human talent of focusing on our partner's part in the relationship while bypassing our own, as well as what we can do to turn this around. Next we'll touch on a vital truth: Turning down the dial does not always weaken our relationship bond, but can strengthen it.

BLISS IS A DIAL WITH A DOWN ARROW . . . AND AN UP ARROW

Let's now traverse some of those places where we can selectively use both turning down and turning up the dial to nourish our relationship.

I See the Best in You

When people turn down the dial on their partner's faults and turn up the dial on their partner's gifts, it forecasts joy in a relationship. Plenty of psychological research speaks to this. People who are merrily wed tend to view their spouse in a shining light, oftentimes even more favorably than their spouse views themselves. They're also more likely to explain away their spouse's unflattering moments, appealing to the outward circumstances at hand (e.g., a bad day), rather than looking inwardly to their character (e.g., grouchy). And when they do think about their partner's flaws, they view them in the context of higher personal strengths and virtues. Take Poppy and Shayne's relationship.

Poppy and Shayne have been happily married for twelve years, and Poppy absolutely adores him. Shayne also has a long history of annoying his friends by making comments that seem self-evident to, well, just about everyone. For example, one evening at a friend's house, Shayne reacts to a movie scene featuring an enraged person by saying, "Wow, she's really mad!" Amid laughter, one of their friends asks Poppy, "Does he do that all the time? How do you put up with that?" Poppy easily replies, "Put up with it? Actually, I've always admired Shayne's total openness and willingness to express exactly what's on his mind."

Notice what Poppy's doing here. For one, she's turning down the dial on Shayne's potentially irritating mannerism. Second, she's seeing him in a more complex, nuanced way than his friends by appreciating his quirk within the larger context of his personal strengths.[38] And her tendency to focus on Shayne's good qualities and turn down the dial on his weak points is likely to nurture her love. People with the strongest tendency to view their partners in a dazzling light are most likely to be happy with their partner. Not only that, they see their relationship discord and uncertainty lessen over the course of one year, effectively transforming the relationship in their mind's eye into a reality.[39] What's more, this kind of glowing outlook predicts relationship fulfillment no matter whether people are married or living together, or whether they're gay, lesbian, or heterosexual.[40]

We're even willing to do some fancy mental tricks to hold on to our praising view of our partner. For instance, a frequent aspect of becoming more intimate is blending our romantic partner into our sense of who we are. People who do this tend to downplay how desirable they think a quality is (e.g., physical appearance, relationship ability) when they think their partner doesn't stack up as well against somebody else on it. By and large, this matches how we treat ourselves, as we can be more inclined to mentally protect ourselves when we compare ourselves to someone else and believe we come up short. So, in essence, when we view our partner's sense of self as joined to our own, a ding to our partner is a ding to us, and we're motivated to repair it.[41]

But even as a sunny outlook on our partner predicts relationship happiness, it also works the other way. For instance, when people write about a delightful relationship moment, as opposed to an unhappy one, they see their partner as being better than themselves when it comes to possessing valuable relationship qualities (e.g., being caring or thoughtful).[42] Essentially, a joyful bond inspires a magnificent vision of our mate.

So does this mean that we should see our loved one only through rosy lenses, turning away from the truth? Definitely not. Relationship happiness is all about balance. Yes, a glowing view of our partner forecasts our enjoyment in the relationship. A greater sense of how much we're alike also predicts bliss, for us and for our partner. All the same, seeing our partner as they see themselves is also crucial in predicting not only our relationship fulfillment but our partner's happiness with us too.[43] As Poppy illustrated, we don't have to choose between seeing the sunshine in our mate and seeing our mate as they are. In fact, we shouldn't choose. If we want to build the closest, most pleasurable and rewarding bond possible, we want to see the best in our partner and truly see them too. When you stop and think about it, this makes good sense. Have you ever felt like someone's take on you didn't fit your own, like they just didn't *get* you? I have, and if you're like most folks, that doesn't feel so hot. No, we gravitate toward those who love us and who can identify our authentic self.

Turning Down the Dial on "Not Tonight, Honey"

"Not tonight, honey; I have a headache." That phrase is so common in pop culture that you probably don't even need me to tell you that it refers to the classic sex refusal excuse. And if you've ever taken a rain check on sex, you're far from alone. Make no mistake, I'm not talking here about those instances when you're in a vulnerable position and are at risk of being taken advantage of by a sexual partner against your will. I'm talking about the garden-variety "just don't really feel like it tonight" refusal of sex with an established intimate partner.

Most people have moments when they just don't quite feel like doing it. But let's take some of the mystery out of this. Is there *anything* that you're raring to do, literally, 100 percent of the time? Do you *always* want to eat, sleep, be social, be alone, exercise, sit, work, play, think, or indulge in mindless pleasures? I'm going to go out on a limb here and assume the answer is no. The same is true for sex. At times when partners are both ready and eager, it's magnificent! But what about those moments when they're not on the same page? Should we always invoke the famed headache? Well, not so much. Recent research demonstrates that even when people aren't totally up for sex, if they feel driven to care for their partner's sexual needs, they can be more likely to turn down the dial on "no" and have sex anyway. And what are the perks of turning down the dial? Both people, including the one who wasn't very excited about having sex in the first place, gets a boost in sexual and relationship happiness. So even though "no" seems like the way to go at times, "yes" holds more potential in the end.

Of course, this definitely doesn't mean that people should always have sex when they don't feel like it. And no one should ever feel forced to have sex when they don't want to. Let's come back to balance. If we only do what we feel like doing and never set that aside to meet our partner's needs, it doesn't set us up for relationship success. By the same token, if we only do what our partner wants, never accounting for our own needs, then we can get into trouble there too.[44] So, in essence, if we're only saying "yes" when the urge for sex burns, we might want to try saying "yes" even when it's more of a smolder.

Toning Down Gripes

Let's be upfront. Stuff happens in life that we don't like. The hassles, the irritations, the vexations: They're part of being human, and sometimes we just want to complain about them, which is totally understandable! But folks don't always like to be on the receiving end of those complaints, so how can we vent our frustrations in a way that doesn't turn people off?

Just as good comedy hinges on delivery, how we deliver a complaint influences how people react to it and to us. When we complain with a dash of humor, we raise the odds that people will find our complaint amusing, will pay more attention to it, and will take a liking to us more. Applying this to our romantic relationship, when we inject humor into some of what we grumble about in life, it'll likely make our complaints more entertaining for our partner to hear and make us more endearing in the process. But there's a limit to the benefit of humor too. If our goal is to share something that's truly bothering us or to reach out for support, then humor is probably going to be counterproductive because it downplays the seriousness of what we're complaining about. In that case, we're less likely to get the reaction we seek.[45] Again, that word *balance* emerges. We can use humor to turn down the dial on the seriousness of our complaints as long as we're OK with our partner minimizing the severity of it too.

Looking back on this stop, we saw that sometimes turning down the dial diminishes the quality of our connection with our partner and brings on the very things we're trying to evade. It can even keep us wavering, agonizingly stuck in a profoundly dissatisfying or unhealthy relationship. Yet it serves us too, helping us to elevate our relationship. We can even turn the dial in both directions: down on our partner's imperfections and up on all of their virtues and greatness. Before we officially end our time on this stop, let's go to the exercises section and put some of what we've gathered to good use.

EXERCISES

Exercise 1: Playing My Part

We explored how we (a) turn down the dial on our sense of vulnerability, (b) wrestle with uncertainty and guard against the heartbreaking possibility of ending a relationship, and (c) bypass our role in troublesome relationship dynamics. In this exercise, you'll have an opportunity to take a look at yourself across these domains. You'll want a separate sheet, either paper or digital. Keep in mind that there's no hurry. You might want to reflect on these questions during walks or other time that you take for yourself, or you could let them bubble way in the back of your mind as you go about your days. Do what's best for you.

1. What are your relationship expectations, and how do they influence how you feel or behave with your partner?
2. Please list at least five ways that you try to guard yourself from vulnerability and the possibility of getting hurt. Do they work for you, against you, or both? If you can, identify one strategy that you'd be willing to change and one small way to begin changing it.
3. If you're in a relationship, how sure are you that your partner is the right one for you? Please use a 0 to 10 scale, where 0 equals not at all sure, and 10 is completely sure. Why did you give the rating you did? If you're unsure about your relationship, what keeps you wanting to stay, and what tempts you to leave? What would you need to make a decision either way and feel good about it?
4. Are there any negative relationship dynamics that you could be playing a role in creating or worsening? Please identify one change that you're willing to make to transform your role into one that's more supportive and good for the relationship.

Exercise 2: Wielding the Dial

On this stop, we explored how we can turn down the dial to uplift the quality of our bond. Now it's time to apply it to your own relationship. You'll want a separate sheet, and, again, there's no rush.

1. Please name at least ten qualities about your partner that you appreciate, admire, or just plain adore. If you don't have a partner right now, think about ten qualities you would value in a partner.

2. Please write about three moments that reflect the greatest, most meaningful times with your partner. Afterward, take stock of how you feel. Do you appreciate your partner more? If so, why?[46]

3. Think of three flaws that have irritated you about your partner, and try fitting them in the grand scheme of your partner's positive qualities, as Poppy did with Shayne. For instance, perhaps your partner's stubbornness reflects their determination, or their slapstick silliness is a side of their wonderful playfulness.

5

DENIAL AT THE LEVEL OF OUR SITUATION

I wonder if being sane means disregarding the chaos that is life, pretending only an infinitesimal segment of it is reality.

—Rabih Alameddine, *Koolaids: The Art of War*

Have you ever traveled by car or plane to a distant, unfamiliar place, trusting that you'd make it to your destination and, though nervous, feeling ready to try something new? Ever taken a new job and felt both excited and apprehensive? What about leaving the home you know and moving someplace else? Perhaps you had those dizzying butterflies, and you felt as though you were standing on the edge of your own personal cliff, unsteady on your feet or unsure which path you wanted to take next in life, but ready to take the leap. This was Lupita's experience.

"Good luck, Lupita!" her friends gleefully cheer, bringing out the cake for her goodbye party. She flashes a broad grin as bittersweet emotions swirled within. The next morning, Lupita hails a taxi to the airport, then boards a plane to her plum job in London. She's never lived anywhere else, but Lupita knows she has to grab this opportunity. Butterflies dance in her stomach as the plane lands. Well, here we go, Lupita. Your whole new life.

If you've ever experienced moments like these, you're far from alone. Yet we sure *feel* alone at these times, don't we? I tend to think of life as a glorious play. Characters enter and exit the stage. A few have starring roles, coming along with us for the lion's share of our story. Others have somewhat lesser roles. And then there are the extras, filling in the background. But we are the lead, the one constant throughout the entire story. We direct how our character responds to events that arise, but that's actually the only thing in the play we can control. And what we do, or don't do, can have dramatic consequences for ourselves, other characters, and the storyline.

As we encounter the complexities and beauty of life, we face decisions that are both unfamiliar and commonplace, in the short term and over the long haul. What's especially thorny is that we can't see into the future, so we're ceaselessly stepping into the dimness of the coming hour, the twilight of tomorrow, and the obscurity of next year. We're always living and choosing with a measure of ignorance. What's more, there's an interaction between what we can and cannot control, the two weaving together and draping a unique fabric over our situation. On top of all that, risk and danger are sewn into the fabric as well. At times, we turn a blind eye to this risk, which has its own ramifications.

How do we make our way in the world, especially with such uncertainty and when there's so much beyond our control? How do we reach for our goals and navigate obstacles amid risk and danger, all the while keeping our wits about us rather than cowering in our bed in a state of panic? On this fourth stop of our tour, we'll explore the multiple ways we turn down the dial on situations we face to pilot the task of living and how this can either pull us down or elevate us. So where shall we begin? Let's start with control.

MY DRIVER'S SEAT, MY SADDLE, AND MY THRONE

One way we turn down the dial on our situation is by assuming that we hold more control over our lives than we do. Why do we do this so readily? We can't boil it down to just one reason, but one factor is that we're constantly motivated to obtain what we desire and ward off what's unpleasant. We even see connections between what we do and the end result when there's no link between the two whatsoever. First-rate examples of this are superstitions, such as wearing a charm for good luck, never walking under a ladder, and staying away from the number thirteen, a number with such significance that a meager 9 percent of Manhattan condominiums with thirteen or more floors actually label the thirteenth floor as the thirteenth floor.[1] As a matter of fact, our craving for control over unpleasant, chance events actually boosts our sense that we're able to evade them, which ultimately heightens our belief that we have more control than we do.[2] We don't want to see ourselves as sitting ducks flapping helplessly in the twisted winds of fate, but as capable, effective conductors of our lives, able to steer toward whatever pleases us while preventing hardship and disaster. So what does this notion of control buy us? What does it cost us?

Excuse Me, This Throne Has a Defect

Sure, a sense of control feels empowering, but that doesn't mean it always serves us. It can also be an appealing hand that seems to give when it actually takes something away. For instance, in investment banking, the more in control traders feel, the less money they bring in and the worse managers judge their work.[3] Here's another work example: The more strongly employees feel a sense of control, the less upset they feel when they believe that their employer is probably going to let them go in the next couple of years—to a point. But beyond an average sense of control, feeling more control is related to more stress among people who think that the end of their job is coming.[4] A false sense of control can arguably fuel addiction too. Consider the classic claim people make that they are in control of their alcohol or other drug use, and capable of stopping it at any time. So a sense of control can be problematic at times. But, whatever you do, don't throw control out the window, because it definitely has its advantages.

Ah, This Saddle Fits Just Right!

A strong dose of control appears to be kind of like a dose of medicine. For instance, it's related to a healthier body and a longer life.[5] In a 2014 study, researchers explored the relationship between physical wellness and a sense of control, which they measured by asking people how much mastery they felt in their life. The idea here is that if we believe that we have the ability to impact elements of life like our physical health, then we're more likely to take steps to improve it, such as exercising more, which pays off for our bodies in variety of ways. And it turns out that a boost in our sense of control is associated with turning back the clock in several areas:[6]

- pulse: four years younger
- "bad" cholesterol: fifteen years younger
- circumference of our midsection: six years younger
- force of our grip: three years younger
- risk for conditions such as cardiovascular disease and diabetes: ten years younger

A greater feeling of control is linked with our emotional health too. For instance, it's connected to our sense of self-respect.[7] It's also one of the three elements of hardiness, an attitude in life that helps us to bravely face difficult situations and find a way to treat them as opportunities for personal development and growth, rather than as troubles that will tear us down. It offers us the spirit and determination to march forward in life. A sense of control is a vital part of all this.[8]

So how can we cultivate a greater sense of control? One way for us to do this is to take on a promotion mind-set. To illustrate this, let's look at the contrast between Dashawn's and Scot's approach to applying to medical school.

Dashawn is a college student dreaming of going to medical school. He's got his eye on any opportunity that will improve his odds of getting in. He's looking forward toward his goal, and he feels excited and energized. This is a promotion mind-set. Meanwhile, Scot also wants to become a physician, but unlike Dashawn, he's more focused on avoiding the possibility of being rejected from medical school. He tenses up with every exam, fearful that he'll do poorly and his grades will slip. In contrast to Dashawn, Scot has more of a prevention mind-set.

In life, we can adopt either of these mind-sets. When we focus on what we want and how we can successfully reach our goals (rather than on preventing mistakes), we nurture a greater sense of control. Importantly, a promotion focus even helps us weather the times when we don't succeed in reaching our goals.[9] In addition to a promotion mind-set, connectedness to others helps too. When we feel like we're part of larger groups of people, such as organizations, communities, or even a nation or the human race, this predicts a greater sense of control, which ultimately forecasts greater wellness for us.[10]

BEAUTIFUL LEAVES, BLOWING IN THE WIND

Now that we've explored the drawbacks and benefits of control, let's consider the flip side. We can assume that we have less control than we do, or carry on without paying attention to where we have control. We can also disregard the long-term consequences of our choices. When we turn down the dial in this manner, we get a mixed bag in return. It can disserve us over time as we dig our own holes, or it can give us a hand as we function day to day. Even the heights of heroism are possible.

The Minuses of Missing Out

We humans have a knack for losing sight of what we can control and how our choices will impact the course of our lives. And we can really get in our own way when this happens. One reason why it occurs is that we simply aren't paying attention.

For example, a good number of people don't think to enroll in their employer's retirement plan even though it will dramatically help them later in life, and only about 6 percent of people reap the benefits of deliberately huffing it up the stairs. But when a simple sign attracts our attention, helping us realize that we have a choice between options, we're much more likely to choose the beneficial one, like taking the stairs rather than the escalator. So what can we do to spot our choices? We can try little prompts of our own, such as smartphone alarms or sticky note signs (e.g., "Take a walk or sit?" "Put some money in a savings account or spend it?").[11] Think about some of the daily choices you have and the kinds of hints you might give yourself to make the healthier ones.

On the other hand, we can be aware that we have a choice but try to avoid making it. Perhaps we don't like any of our options, or we don't know which one is best, so we hold off, thinking that we're sparing ourselves from deciding. But what we lose sight of is that with every day we hold off making a choice, we are essentially choosing to keep things the same.[12] Take Rikki's situation.

Rikki doesn't know whether to leave her job in New York City and take another one in San Francisco, or remain where she is. Gripped with fear that she'd make the "wrong" choice, she avoids the decision. Three years later, she is still in the same job in New York. She thought she evaded a choice, yet she's been choosing all along.

In all likelihood, most of us have been in Rikki's shoes at some point. And that's not inherently a problem either, as long as we don't lull ourselves into the false sense of security that we can dodge choices. Every day, we vote with our behavior to change something or hold on to it.

And we have plenty of other ways we unwittingly exit the driver's seat of our lives. Let's explore a few others.

Spending

Ever felt your eyes bulge out of their sockets when the cashier told you how much your groceries cost? Plenty of us have been there. It can be easy to marvel at how money just flies away, but the good news is that we have more control than we think over that grocery bill. We're more likely to buy extras that aren't on our shopping list the longer we're in the store and when we exceed our originally planned budget.[13] When we stick to a budget and resist the temptation to wander those aisles, we'll be able to keep a little extra cash in our pocket.

Addiction

Just as some people reassure themselves that they're in total control of their alcohol and other drug use even when they're not, the reverse can also happen. A sense of having too little control over alcohol use is linked to struggles with drinking.[14] Many believe they're locked in the firm grip of addiction with no hope of a way out. A number of people think they're not capable of handling life's stressors and that they "need" alcohol or drugs to carry on. Then they descend even deeper into addiction. For instance, binge drinking, which translates into five drinks for men and four drinks for women in a single sitting, is associated with stressful life experiences, denial, and the use of other drugs to manage stress.[15] And among people who have had a traumatic experience, the belief that they don't have control over their healing process is related to struggling with symptoms of PTSD, which itself is linked to turning to alcohol to get by. Sadly, as we've talked about before, this strategy gives with one hand by numbing the pain, and takes with the other by paving the way for an alcohol use disorder.[16]

If you think you might need help, countless people know what you're going through. What's more, they know the freedom that comes with getting help and climbing out of the hole of addiction. And if you're trying to help someone who's struggling, please know that there are multiple ways to reach a better place, and even if that person resists the treatment options recommended by their doctor, it pays to explore other options.[17]

The Stressful Cards Life Deals

After life deals a major blow, we can feel like we're thrown up against a wall, with no control over our circumstances—and maybe that's true. But it's also possible that we have choices but don't believe we do, and so we remain stuck.

Intimate partner violence is a powerful, tragic example of this, and it happens far more often than people think. According to the National Intimate Partner and Sexual Violence Survey, in any given *minute,* twenty men and women in the United States are enduring violence at the hands of their romantic partner. That means that in just five minutes from the time you read this sentence, one hundred men and women will face danger and fear in a situation that should embody love and safety. In a year from now, we're talking about ten million people.[18] What's more, roughly 64 percent of people, on average, who experience violence in their relationship will go on to develop PTSD, with PTSD becoming more likely as the violence occurs more often.[19] Sadly, one barrier that can prevent people from leaving a violent partner is denial of the true nature of the situation, which can take multiple forms. People can turn down the dial on their partner's accountability for the abuse, blame themselves, downplay the abuse, or distort their reasons for staying.

For example, a man may bear his wife's repeated hits and punches in secret, telling himself that he has no right to complain about abuse from a woman, even after she breaks his arm. No matter what form it takes, the tragic end result is that people in this situation don't always see the choice to leave. On top of that, many men and women who use violence in their relationship find ways to turn down the dial on what's happening to condone their actions,[20] which maintains the abuse—such as a husband who justifies striking his wife by telling her that, if she'd just stop nagging, she wouldn't force him to do it.

Bullying is another context where people can feel trapped. The classic example is the schoolyard bully, but adult workplace bullies also exist. Estimates of the percentage of people who say that bullying occurs in their workplace stretch from 2 percent to 27 percent. Examples of workplace bullying include mocking, bad-mouthing, rejection, discrimination, physical harm, and sexual coercion. In response to workplace bullying, some people try to crank the dial on their situation way down by turning to alcohol, acting as though everything is fine, or focusing on the pleasing parts of their job rather than exploring their options to change the situation. This is an entirely understandable response, especially when it seems like there's no choice in the matter. The problem is that it's linked to additional troubles, as people who cope with workplace bullying in this way are more likely to struggle with lowered psychological and physical health and to take more days off work.[21]

Having health difficulties is another stressful situation in which we can turn away from the options available to us. For example, as people age, some may face challenges with their ability to move around as they'd like, such as being more likely to fall or having a tougher time walking. Yet people don't always choose to get help. One reason for this is that they reject the notion that they need help at all,[22] leaving them frozen in the situation. On the other hand, when people see where they can exert control over a disability or illness and make choices, the storm of stress becomes a little more manageable. For instance, women with breast cancer who convey their treatment wishes more often while discussing pre-surgery options feel a greater sense of vigor and morale, and less apprehension and worry.[23]

The Plusses of Passing Up

Up to this point, we've been exploring the drawbacks of disregarding control and the consequences of our choices. But what about the upside of doing so? Let's touch on a couple of these.

Defying a Painful Choice

Most of us will at some time have to make a significant, agonizingly painful choice, but as long as we don't have to make it right now, we'll turn away from it as much as we can. Arguably, this form of turning down the dial helps us function day to day without falling apart. Examples of painful choices include the decision to put a loved one in a hospital or a nursing home against their will, to exclude someone from our lives if they hurt us one more time, to euthanize a dying pet, or to stop driving as our eyesight or reflexes deteriorate. This latter decision is one that confronts many people in industrialized nations as they age. After a life of independence with a car, the decision to stop driving can be an immensely bitter pill to swallow. For some, the ability to focus on going about their daily lives and deny that they will have to make that choice feels like a godsend.[24]

Defying Danger

Downplaying the long-term consequences of our actions can allow us to engage in feats of heroism. Ordinarily, when we think of heroism, we picture someone charging into harm's way to assist another, often at notable personal risk. Lewis Thomas is an excellent example of this. In 1996, he confronted two gunmen on a subway while they robbed and pummeled three teenagers, and they shot him in the process. Thankfully, he survived and received the Carnegie Medal.[25] Heroes like Mr. Thomas tend to act spontaneously and probably don't think much about the possible consequences of their bravery before acting.[26] But heroic acts can stretch out over time, not just happen in a flash.[27] Consider those brave few who protected the lives of Jewish people during the

Holocaust despite overwhelming personal risk to themselves and their families. Even though these courageous men and women had more time to think through their decision, and many had strong principles fueling their actions, they still had to be willing to take a dramatic chance.[28] Presumably, they needed to turn down the dial on the possibility that they and their families could actually lose their lives.

On the whole, when we turn down the dial on our ability to make choices or on the possible consequences of our actions, it can trap us in misery. At the same time, it can also help us carry on and even save others in the face of overwhelming risk. Yet, believe it or not, risk is far more pervasive in daily life than in dramatic moments of heroism. Coming up next, we'll explore the ways we turn the dial down on risk and how we can either benefit or sabotage ourselves in the process.

RISKY BUSINESS? NOT HERE!

As we go about living, we carry along a set of beliefs that lead us to downplay our sense of risk and vulnerability to harm. They include notions such as the following:

- People are basically decent, and bad things probably aren't going to happen to us.
- Life is generally fair, so as long as we're decent and try to do the right thing, we'll be fine. The cliché "you reap what you sow" reflects this idea.
- As long as we make prudent choices, we can control what happens to us and can safeguard ourselves against harm.

Of course, not all of us hold these beliefs, particularly if we've encountered seriously harmful or damaging experiences that defy these ideas,[29] but many of us do. So what does this sense of being almost risk-proof give us? And how can it cost us? Let's start with the price we pay in a few areas.

It's Risky to Turn Down the Dial on Risk

Driving

Let's come back to Lupita's journey. She focused on the risks of a major move and a job change. Yet, risk research reveals that she actually took her biggest chance on the drive to the airport, and she didn't think a second thought about it. We're actually just as likely to die on a cross-country flight between Los Angeles and Boston as we are driving a measly twelve miles by car. Yet many of us fearlessly drive every day, and the consequences can be tragic. Study findings reveal that in the year following the terrorist attacks of September 11, 2001, the number of people who drove sharply bumped up. Presumably, this reflected people's decision to drive rather than fly in an attempt to avoid facing the same doom as the 256 passengers who lost their lives on the four planes that horrific day. Terribly, it backfired, and approximately 1,500 additional people died on the roads during that year in the mistaken belief that they were making themselves safer.[30]

Alcohol

Although anyone can struggle with their drinking, some are more at risk than others. For instance, there's ample scientific evidence that people with a family history of alcohol addiction are especially at risk of developing a drinking problem, but not everyone with a family history acknowledges their risk. This is unfortunate, because an awareness of their risk predicts lowered alcohol use.[31] But regardless of family history, it's unsafe to minimize the risks around alcohol. For example, people who make light of their likelihood of having difficulties linked to drinking in college, such as conflicts over alcohol use, are actually at greater odds of experiencing these types of problems.[32]

Health

We're also experts at playing down health risks. Unfortunately, this can also lessen our odds of taking preventive measures or inflate the chances that we'll miss the full scope of our risk. For instance, a 2014 study reveals that people who are obese believe they're more likely to have a stroke or a heart attack than they really are, yet they downplay their odds of battling hypertension and rheumatism.[33] Among women with higher odds of developing breast cancer, a whopping 89 percent of them underplay their risk.[34] And people who tend to believe that bad stuff probably won't happen to them are more likely to minimize their risk for cardiovascular disease and are less inclined to take preventive measures.[35]

Then Again, It's Risky Not to Turn Down the Dial on Risk

Despite the disadvantages of turning down the dial on risk, denial of risk is also a potent helpmate. For instance, people who make light of the odds of bad things befalling them, even after a cardiac health scare, are actually less likely to experience another scare again in the coming year.[36] And even among people who think aging means having less health and vitality—a mind-set that itself is a risk factor for health problems over time—an upbeat, confident vision of the future can help safeguard people's mental and physical health over time as they age.[37]

What's more, our ability to turn down the dial on risk arguably helps sustain us as we travel the road of life and reach for our goals, which is a journey filled with uncertainty. If we're going to embrace that journey, we probably need to be willing to take chances and downplay the risks. Lupita is a shining example. If she truly believed that she'd fail miserably at her job and hate London, she wouldn't have tried it, right? When we turn down the dial on risk, it's like giving ourselves a mental safety net. It bolsters us to live our lives, to get out of bed and function throughout our day, rather than cower under the covers in terror at all of the potential hazards awaiting us. It allows us to be healthy, engaged human beings in the world and to go after the gems that life has to offer. We might just want to remind ourselves that we're not invincible either, and to be grateful for what we have in life for as long as we have it.

I'LL GET TO IT . . . A LITTLE LATER

When we think of choices, it's easy to picture what we actually do, but choices also involve what we put off. Just as we humans spring with eagerness toward our passions and the pleasures we relish, we have a flair for turning down the dial on tasks we don't want to do. It's called procrastination, and we're heading there now—without delay.

The temptation to put off to tomorrow what we don't want to do today is completely human, understandable, and quite common. There is zero judgment coming from me! Roughly 20 percent of adults and 50 percent of college students do it. And in the short term, procrastination eases the stress of having to do the undesirable. Still, it costs us more in the long run than just getting right down to what we need to do. It's associated with diminished physical and psychological health, lower academic and career achievement, higher levels of stress on the job, and reduced financial security.[38]

Considering all the problems it brings, what causes procrastination and how can we turn things around so we don't do it, at least not as much? For one, research suggests that there's a link between procrastinating and paying attention to the present moment rather than the future, and that stress is related to the time frame where people place their attention. To be sure, ordinarily it's highly adaptive to zero in on the here and now when we're facing stress. How can we handle the difficulties, pickles, and messes that require attention today if we're focused on tomorrow? Thankfully, our brains and bodies are built to make this needed shift in focus for our welfare! But what about when the stress we're facing doesn't involve adversity or an urgent hardship, but a bothersome task that we have to do yet would really love to throw overboard? In that case, evading it is probably not going to work. If anything, it'll most likely just hand us a heaping spoonful of stress and trouble down the road when we're scurrying to get that task done at the last minute or too late. So, if you're one of the many who is tempted to procrastinate to lighten stress right now, instead try finding other ways to relieve stress and consider how much less stressed you'll feel later on, not to mention how much better you'll perform your task if you start now.[39] Similarly, another factor associated with procrastination is being tired and having a tough time mentally separating from work and taking downtime from the demands of the job.[40] So consider occasionally re-evaluating how much you're working, as well as your current lifestyle and self-care routine.

So far, we've pored over the assorted ways we can turn down the dial on our situation. We can minimize our lack of control, disregard choices or the eventual consequences, underestimate danger, and let unappealing tasks slide. But we're also skilled at turning down the dial on another disagreeable feature of our situation: inconsistencies. Our behavior doesn't always match what we believe.

DO AS I THINK, NOT AS I DO

How do our beliefs and our behavior dance out of step? You name it. For one, we can deny that an issue applies to us. One remarkable example comes from a study showing that roughly 56 percent of the college students who smoked cigarettes a few times per month claimed they weren't smokers, and just over 9 percent said the same even though they smoked either every day or every other day![41] We can also justify all sorts of behaviors that we don't approve of by rejecting responsibility for our actions,[42] such as blaming a stressful job for our problem drinking or pinning angry outbursts on how someone else "makes" us feel. Additionally, we can praise actions that others do, yet we fall short in doing them ourselves. For example, we applaud people who tackle large public problems (e.g., social injustice) but lean toward doing nothing ourselves if we don't think it's a productive way to spend our time.[43]

When we become aware of these mismatches between our beliefs and our actions, we feel unsettled and want to lighten that tension. This is known as *cognitive dissonance.* So we turn down the dial on this inconsistency, allowing us to feel more at ease.[44] In some cases, this can lead us to maintain the status quo and continue doing what we're doing. However, it can also help us change. For instance, when researchers in a 2015 study asked supermarket shoppers to sign a poster against using plastic bags, these shoppers were far less likely to use plastic bags later when they had the chance.[45] They had already taken a public position against using plastic bags, and this likely motivated them to behave consistently.

Can you think of inconsistencies between your beliefs and your actions? If you can, it just makes you human. We all do it. Fortunately, we can use our awareness of these inner mismatches to mature and flourish. On this next and final leg of our stop, we're going to examine what we believe a little more, specifically the way we view our situations.

IF THE OUTLOOK FITS, WEAR IT

We have an overall outlook on life—a lens—that influences the way we understand our situation. We've got our own glaze that we pour over what happens in life, and we don't often consider that this layer might not reflect reality, or that there's more than one way to see a situation. And this lens holds the potential to lift us up or drain us, depending upon which lens we use.

Getting Hemmed In

Just because a viewpoint is ours doesn't mean it's good for us. At times, when we unquestioningly buy into our own frame of reference, we risk getting trapped in continued pain or ill-suited patterns. Take Quinn's tragic situation.

> *Quinn never really thought much about his safety until a mass shooting happened at his university, resulting in the loss of a dear friend. On that horrifying day, his whole world turned upside down. Now, he sees life as more dangerous, unpredictable, and less purposeful, and he sees himself as a helpless passenger.*

Sadly, others share Quinn's story. According to a 2015 study on the impact of the Virginia Tech mass shooting, people with more intense post-traumatic stress symptoms were more likely to see themselves as less competent, and their lives as more unsafe and less purposeful. Individuals with this changed perspective were also more likely to feel deeper grief one year after the shooting.[46]

A cynical view is another perspective that can work against us. In fact, people with a cynical outlook on human nature are likely to make less money or to miss out on making more money over the course of nine years compared to people without this frame of mind. All the same, it's worth noting that this viewpoint is only a disadvantage in places where widespread suspicion of others probably isn't justified.[47]

Another notion about human nature that can potentially undermine us is that people don't have free will. It's been shown that when individuals are led to think there's no free will, they don't have as much trust in the genuine thoughtfulness of other people, and are not as grateful for others' giving deeds. This makes sense when we stop and think about it. Our ability to be grateful to people hinges on our belief that they freely and honestly choose to do us a good turn, with no concealed motives. If we remove that, we erode our ability to appreciate their kindnesses.[48] Do we really want a life with that way of looking at human nature? Probably not! On the other hand, there are angles we *can* take on life that a lot of us might want.

Flowing Nicely

Just as it can hinder us to see ourselves as smaller after trauma, the flip side of this is that, in the wake of trauma—even a major event like witnessing a mass shooting, surviving an accident, or being the victim of a crime—people can identify ways they evolved and grew afterward. This way of thinking is known as post-traumatic growth. And people with this viewpoint are more likely to see themselves as competent and resourceful, to look forward to the future, and to envision what's significant and purposeful in life.[49]

Another lens we wear in life is how we think about mistakes. Do you see mistakes as pitfalls you have to evade whenever possible, or are they windows for growth and wisdom? My mother always used to tell me, "Mistakes are OK. Just focus on learning from them." She was more right than she realized. The mind-set that mistakes offer chances to learn is linked to a greater sense of competence and a better ability to look after our own process of learning. So when we treat mistakes as opportunities to learn and grow, we increase the odds that we'll actually learn and grow from them.[50]

On this stop, we learned that free will helps us hold on to gratitude. But what other benefits are linked to gratitude? Quite a few. For instance, people who feel extensive gratitude are also likely to handle stress more effectively, to have greater support from their network of loved ones, to be more contented in their lives, and to feel less distressed.[51]

At previous stops on our tour, we talked about how we can turn down the dial with an uplifting frame of mind. That certainly applies here at the level of our situation. For instance, an exceedingly common experience for working men and women is the challenge of effectively balancing home and job life. Career can run over into family life and vice versa, and this mutual interference can undermine psychological health and happiness. Fortunately, a more encouraging point of view that spots the advantages in straddling these two worlds can help us continue taking care of our life and developing as a person. For example, you can see the challenge of juggling it all as a stepping stone to more career opportunities and to another way of helping your family.[52]

Now that we've sorted through some of the ways that the lens we use influences how we feel and experience situations in life, it's almost time to wind down this stop on our tour. Before we leave, we'll introduce exercises that you can use to bring what we've explored here to life, and then we'll take off for our next stop at the level of society.

EXERCISES

Exercise 1: The Long and Short of It

On this stop, we learned that our viewpoint on situations has a powerful impact on how we feel and how we respond to them. At times, our outlook serves us. At others, it limits our quality of life. The tricky part is that we can get so caught up in the view through our own lens that we don't even realize there's another perspective that we could take. This exercise is designed to help you catch the stories you tell yourself that hold you back in some way (don't worry—we all have them!), and to begin to cultivate a new point of view that supports you. You'll want a separate sheet for this exercise, be it paper or digital. And just remember, there's no right or wrong answer here. The key is to be authentic and to use lenses that work for *you.*

1. Take some time and reflect upon your circumstances in life right now, and then answer the questions below:
    - Imagine that you're talking to a good, supportive friend. What would they tell you about your ability to handle your life right now? What encouraging words or pieces of wisdom would they offer?

- What mistakes do you find yourself consistently making? How do you feel about mistakes?
- Now, please identify the upside of your mistakes, namely the lessons that you could learn from them. How could these lessons help you to grow and become a better person?

2. Make a list with three columns. In the first column, please write anything that's going on in your life that you don't like. It can be little things (e.g., traffic) all the way to the big stuff (e.g., a painful loss). In the second column, please write what it is about each item that you don't like (e.g., traffic holds me up from getting home when I want). Now, in the third column, please write down any possible benefits or silver linings, no matter how small, you can see from the situation (e.g., in traffic, I have more time to reflect upon my life). Just to be clear, if you identify a plus side to an upsetting situation, this does not mean that you're glad it occurred. It only means you recognize that not everything that came out of the situation was terrible. For example, after an extremely stressful experience, some people say it helped them realize that they're stronger than they thought they were, or that they reprioritized their life and saw what's really important.

We've been exploring the challenges and the downsides in your present situation. Now, let's look at the other side—what you're grateful for in your life.

3. Make a list of as many things you're grateful for as possible. You can even group them into categories if you want, such as the people you care about and what you appreciate about them, aspects of your life that you're thankful for (e.g., where you live, the job you have, your health), and the little things (e.g., French vanilla coffee, Sunday afternoon football, and the brilliant colors of fall leaves). And remember not to leave yourself out! Include any talents, characteristics, and abilities that you possess and are thankful for. And then, think about and jot down why you're grateful for each item on your list.

Exercise 2: Steering Our Own Ship

On this stop, we explored how we sometimes overlook places where we can control the course of life more than we do, and how this can lead us to flounder in unfavorable circumstances or even entrench us deeper into difficulty. Of course, this doesn't mean that we cause all of our own troubles. We certainly don't! However, once the troubles are at our doorstep, no matter what their cause may be, we must manage them, and it's here where we can unintentionally hold ourselves back from healing and living a more gratifying, fulfilling life. In this exercise, you'll have an opportunity to identify how you could be fueling the hardships you're facing, as well as what changes might allow you to step closer to what you want over time. You'll also want a separate sheet for your answers.

1. Make a list of some of the problems you're facing right now that are interfering with your ability to fully enjoy life. For any problem, please identify at least one way that you contribute to it in some fashion. The goal here is not to beat up on yourself but to empower yourself by grabbing on to what you can control—your own responses. You might want to consider ways that you're causing the situation to feel more upsetting or at least not any better. For example, let's say you're feeling deeply distressed because a relative just died. In response, you're isolating yourself from friends and loved ones, and you're drinking more than usual. Your avoidance of people and steeper alcohol use are two ways you would be unknowingly leading yourself toward feeling worse or not helping yourself to heal.

2. As a follow-up to the previous question, please write down one choice you can make that will either help you to improve the problem or prevent you from making it any worse. In the example above, you might decide to call a friend and ask them out to dinner. Or perhaps one night you might go to the gym or watch a comedy rather than numb your feelings with alcohol.

3. We all have times when our actions and ideas don't go together. Please identify three beliefs or ideas that you hold but don't actually follow. For example, you might heartily believe that it's

important to exercise, eat well, get enough sleep, recycle, give to charity, speak kindly to people, and refrain from gossip, but you might not necessarily do these things. It might not feel so great to do this part of the exercise, but just remember, all humans have inconsistencies like these, so go easy on yourself. Next, please write down one way, no matter how small, that you're willing to bring your behavior more in line with your beliefs. For instance, if you're not exercising at all, you might buy a pedometer and start walking ten minutes per day.

4. Picture the life you want five years from now. What does it look like? There are lots of questions you can ponder to get at this: What kind of person are you? How are you feeling? How are you spending your time? What goals, be they personal or professional, have you accomplished? What kinds of things are you doing to care for yourself? What's your outlook on yourself and the world? What lessons have you learned? As you do this part of the exercise, remember to be realistic. For example, you can't grant yourself magic powers, as cool as that would be! But at the same time, don't sell yourself short and assume you'll never be able to attain a major goal in that time frame. For instance, if you picture being in much better physical health and completing a marathon in five years, give yourself permission to write it down![53]

5. Then think backward and write down what you would need to do to reach this vision. Would it involve a change in outlook or habits, or other major changes in your lifestyle or career? Once you've got this down, please write three specific things you would be willing to start doing right now to advance toward what you want.

6

DENIAL AT THE LEVEL OF SOCIETY

The thing about denial is that it doesn't feel like denial when it's going on.

—Georgina Kleege, *Sight Unseen*

Welcome to stop number five, denial at the level of society. On this stop, we're going to explore three main aspects of social life where we turn down the dial on the undesirable. And even though we are separating them out into discrete segments on this journey, don't be fooled. They mingle together all around us, sometimes in ways we don't notice. In the following example, Jules encounters all of them as she goes about her day.

Jules tunes into her favorite morning show to add a little humor to her day. She hears something else. "I'll tell you," the radio host comments flatly, "there are some female comediennes who are funny, but by and large, women just can't tell a joke." Jules turned it off, her vigor flattened.

Later, her team of fellow partners discuss whether to take on a high-profile new law case. Jules thinks, This case is a three-ring disaster! Most of these guys don't want to take it, so this is gonna be over in a snap. *"OK, everyone," one of the partners says, "I know it's going to be a tough fight and the odds of winning are slim, but that's what this firm is all about.*

Who's with me?" Jules sits, stupefied, as all of the other hands in the room systematically rise up. "So, what's your vote, Jules?" Shame and nervousness flood her as she waveringly raises her hand too, thinking, I can't be the only one to say no, especially being the only woman. I'd look like I'm not strong enough to handle this.

Later that night, she and her fiancé, Zac, a university professor, exchange the day's updates at their favorite steakhouse. "Honestly, I feel so stilted sometimes, afraid that anything I do will get twisted as 'typical' female behavior," Jules grumbles.

"I feel that way too," Zac says thoughtfully. "I'm the only Black professor in the department, surrounded by White faculty, and there's always a little part of me that's frightened I'll confirm a stereotype." As they gaze at each other with newfound understanding, the restaurant bill's arrival breaks the silence. Zac places his credit card on the tray, the two of them mindless of doing it any other way.

In the first segment of this chapter, we'll delve into how other people's beliefs and actions powerfully sway us. We want to envision ourselves charting our own course through life, yet other people steer us far more than we'd like to think. An illustration of this was when Jules and her law partners all followed along with one another in lockstep.

Next, in the second leg of our stop, we'll look at our penchant for turning down the dial on large-scale problems and the suffering of others. For example, while Jules and Zac attuned to each other's struggles, they remained blissfully unaware of the suffering animals endured before becoming steaks on their dinner plate that night.

Then, in the third part, we'll explore the *isms* that turn down the dial on equality. These isms (e.g., racism, sexism) can take the form of prejudiced attitudes (e.g., thinking less of some groups) as well as discrimination (e.g., unfair hiring decisions). We'll touch on how isms affect everyone, regardless of whether they are on the giving or receiving end of them. We'll also look at our denial of the isms themselves, as well as strategies we can use to counteract them. In light of the many isms in society, unfortunately, we only have space to explore a few, and I sincerely apologize in advance if I leave out ones that of are personal concern for you. Exercises at the end will give you an opportunity to explore features of our stop in your own life. Whenever you're ready, let's navigate into society.

FITTING IN

Here are two things we can't deny about ourselves:

1. We love to feel like we have a sense of control over our choices and our lives.
2. We are profoundly social creatures.

Now, on the face of it, it might be tempting to think that our control and our social world can coexist without really affecting each other. After all, we want to see ourselves as completely self-governing. It's almost irresistible to believe that we can gather into social circles with people; form relationships with them; share space, money, food, power, time, and opportunities; *and* have a freewheeling hand over our daily lives, but stay beyond the sphere of other people's influence. Is this an understandable wish? For sure! Is it accurate? Eh, not so much. People in our social world influence us deeply, far more than we realize, and we're about to look through a few of the stunning ways they do so. Some are for our betterment, whereas others can hinder us. But a lot of them, in all likelihood, fly right under our notice.

Why We Go Along

We conform to other people, meaning that we alter our actions in some way because of others.[1] And we do so for two superb reasons:

1. We want to get the lowdown on what's going on around us so we can make the right choices.
2. We want others to like us and accept us. We want to feel like we fit in with people, rather than be alone.[2]

Essentially, we turn to each other for information and relationships. It's a brilliant strategy! First, people can offer vital clues on how to successfully navigate a situation.[3] To illustrate, imagine that you landed on another planet amid an alien population that looked just like humans. How would you know what customs to follow or how to distinguish what's dangerous from what's benign? The aliens around you would be an ideal place to start!

Second, we're pretty much made to be socially joined with others. And besides, to borrow the cliché, there's safety in numbers. Let's say that you didn't fit in with society, and the powers that be completely banished you (a dismal idea, I know). No medical help, supplies, or protection. If you're like most of us, you wouldn't last long. How do you prevent this? Follow along with what the group likes, rather than tip the applecart and turn people off. So truly, we need each other. And we pay close attention to one another. For instance, other people's reactions influence how much we delight in various experiences in our lives.[4] We even take a liking to goods more when we see other people merely eyeing them, never mind buying them. It's in the eyes; they easily affect us.[5]

Showing Ourselves

Not only can people impact what we prefer, but they can also affect how we express ourselves. Take the Spanish city of Barcelona, for example. Many people there and elsewhere in Spain speak a language known as Catalan, and a number of Catalan people want to secede from Spain. Some of them express their support for independence by hanging a Catalan flag on the front of their home. You can see these flags scattered about Barcelona, but they're not dispersed evenly. Instead, they appear in batches, presumably based on what others who live nearby are doing. People are apt to lay out a flag if plenty of other people nearby are, and they are less likely to do so if most folks around them aren't.[6]

How others behave also bears upon what we think we ought to do. For instance, we base our sense of how much money we think we should give to others on how much money others are doling out. As people give more, we think we ought to do likewise. Unfortunately, the reverse is also true. We feel less obligated to chip in as we see others' generosity lessen.[7] A similar dynamic plays out with how much we exert ourselves. When we don't think the odds of success are high, we're inclined to match our efforts to what we believe others are doing, whether that's to rein ourselves in or give it our best shot.[8] But we don't need to see a whole group of people going all out to boost our own desire to try harder. As a matter of fact, just one person in a work team who gives it their all can elevate the whole team's performance as long as that person plays a pivotal role, and offers ideas and assistance to others on the team.[9]

Shaping Our Habits

We also go along with others in our habits. For instance, lots of us are accustomed to using our own cars to get around. Researchers in a 2015 study asked people to drive their cars 25 percent less often and then gave some of them an exaggerated idea of how many other folks were switching to more environmentally friendly commuting habits. Would we ever exchange the overwhelming convenience of driving our personal car to mimic others? Absolutely. People who got the inflated information used their own cars to get to work about *five times* less often! Although the goal of driving 25 percent less may have also motivated people to change, the fact that they remodeled their commuting habits in line with what they believed others were doing points to the potent role of our social world in molding how we live.[10]

Alcohol use is another example. People's belief that it's commonplace not to drink alcohol predicts a more positive image of those who don't drink, which in turn forecasts less drinking.[11] On the other hand, in the world of sales, accepted practices of drinking during work meetings are linked to how much new employees and clients believe that drinking can boost their careers, which predicts higher levels of drinking.[12] But what's especially thorny about social influence and alcohol use is that, as a 2014 study reveals, not only do people drink more when the people around them do, most of the time they won't even realize that others are affecting how much they're drinking.[13]

Pulling Strings on the Little Things

People have incredible, highly subtle ways of impacting each other. Many of these ways are unintentional, and other ways aren't. There are a number of examples. For instance, when we're new to a group, people are more inclined to like us when we use pronouns that portray us as part of the group (e.g., *we* and *us*) rather than ones that set us apart (e.g., *I* or *me*).[14] People in our social life also impact what we remember and forget about the past based on what details they include and leave out when they talk about it.[15] Additionally, people influence the emotional power of our unpleasant memories. When we share an upsetting memory with someone who is a responsive listener, our memory's emotional force dwindles in short order, like air escaping a balloon. Unfortunately, the opposite is true if we're talking to someone who's not as engaged (e.g., listening without commenting on what we're sharing in any way).[16] In this case, the distress we feel intensifies soon afterward. However, the effect is temporary.

Arya's disagreeable day offers us an illustration.

On her way home from work, Arya listens to the radio while she is stuck in traffic. Her eyes flick up to the rearview mirror just in time to see a car approaching too rapidly for comfort. She braces herself for the forceful slam that rocks her from behind. As Mackenzie, the other driver, emerges from her luxury car, additional unpleasantness follows.

"This is all your fault!" Mackenzie shouts. "If your car had been a little farther up, this would never have happened, and my lawyers will make sure that your insurance company pays for everything!"

Although Arya is grateful to be uninjured (aside from a stiff neck and a headache), the ordeal was nerve-racking all the same, and she can't resist telling her colleague, Lori, about it the following day. As Arya gives her run-down on what happened, Lori listens placidly without breaking her silence—not a "that's awful!" or a "so what happened next?" to be had. As Arya shuts the door of her office, the jitteriness, irritation, and general unease she'd been carrying that day bubbles up.

What's more, our social environment can even unconsciously impact our ability to read other people's emotions. For example, we're better at spotting fear in another person when someone else is looking at them angrily, even if we can't pick up on the angry person's presence consciously.[17]

On top of all that, people purposefully try to influence us at times with techniques that can slip right under our radar. One of these is called the "foot in the door" approach. Specifically, when we go along with a minor request, this ups the odds that we'll do the same with a bigger request down the road. This works so well that even when someone asks us for a small favor like telling them the time, we're inclined to do more for them later. One study showed that a simple favor like lending someone a hand with directions can actually increase the odds of that person being open to getting together.[18] Another approach is called "evoking freedom." When someone asks us to do something while reminding us of our liberty to say no, ironically, we're more apt to say yes. That's true even when it means complying with something we wouldn't normally be comfortable doing.[19] We even alter our behavior when we think that others are watching us, regardless of whether the eyes watching us are real. For instance, here's an easy way to increase the amount of money people put into a shared pool, such as a workplace fund for coffee. It turns out that some paper, a pen, and a little tape to construct a pair of eyes are a handy solution. People will contribute more for that fund at work when the collection box has paper eyes on it. And this tactic works in advertising too. Print ads that ask us whether we'll buy environmentally sound products are more persuasive when they feature an image of a person looking straight at us.[20]

Being Good for Us

Even as some social influences pull our strings in the wrong direction, they can brighten our health and wellness too. In the short term, as we discussed a little earlier, a responsive and active listener soothes the emotional power of unsettling memories. Over time, the caring support others give us serves as a cushion against stress and is also linked to our contentment with life. In this technology-driven age, it may be tempting to think that support from our online buddies is sufficient, but we might want to reconsider that. Some research has shown that online support, a common facet of many people's lives, doesn't seem to have the same effect.[21]

But the benefits of other people's influence on us get even more dramatic. It's been shown that we're at greater risk for dementia when we don't have a close friend to talk to, even when we take age out of the equation.[22] On top of all that, a social life appears to save our life—literally. A 2015 study compiled the results of seventy other studies and over three million people, and revealed that when we are solitary and lonesome, we're almost 30 percent more likely to die within the next seven years, even after accounting for other factors that would forecast our death.[23]

So, on the whole, a willingness to band together with people and to let others influence us is an exceedingly healthy way to go through life. The key, once again, is to strike a balance. Where the pull of other people can brighten us, we do well to follow. And where it's liable to hinder us, we might not. But how do we catch people's influence on us when it can be thorny to pinpoint? We can't always spot it, but we can certainly try. When we pay attention, thoughtfully reflect on what other people are saying, and tune in to what we sincerely think and feel, we'll be more effective in accepting influence when we truly want to do so.[24] And just the mere awareness that people impact us can help us to notice these moments of influence more effectively. For instance, when I teach my social psychology course, I love to show my students the Old Spice commercial with the man on the horse with diamonds in his hands. (Search for "Old Spice, I'm on a horse" on YouTube.) If you haven't seen it, you really should. It tells us nothing whatsoever about the product, but it's hilarious. And that's the whole point. It reflects a technique called *the soft sell,* and its aim is to make us laugh and connect cheery feelings with the product (not to mention the attractive actor), upping our odds of buying it.[25] If I hadn't known about the ways people influence us, I wouldn't have picked up on it in this commercial. But I did know, and now you do too!

To recap this leg of our tour, we explored the tremendous extent of social influence despite our wish to hold on to the notion that we think and act more independently than we do. In this second part of our stop, we're going to touch on how we turn away from more expansive social issues, another way we turn down the dial in society.

TUNING OUT

We're capable of great love, caring, and giving, but we're also adept at turning down the dial on pervasive challenges, including others' suffering. So if you identify with Giles in the following example, please cut yourself some slack—and join the rest of society.

> *After a long slog at work, Giles can't wait for a tranquil evening with the TV.* Ah! There it is! *he eagerly thinks as he finds*

a movie he wants to see. Then a commercial break interrupts his tranquility. "Every day, countless people die of starvation," a voice laments as haunting images of emaciated faces and bodies pan across his television screen. "Oh no," Giles groans, getting up to grab something to drink and avoid what he is seeing. "Not right now."

We all find ourselves distanced from others' hurt at times. And this isn't necessarily unhealthy either. Just imagine if we could feel the totality of the suffering in the world. We'd either lose our minds or we'd sob all day, too despondent and hopeless to get out of bed. So, just as we've seen on the other stops of our tour, we need the ability to turn the dial both ways: up and down. Here, though, we're going to focus our attention on when we turn down the dial a little too far.

Giving Human Suffering the Slip

The study of how we turn away from others' suffering is gripping. Dr. Stanley Cohen, a sociologist, outlined three categories of this form of denial. The first type is when we say that a problem simply isn't there. Those who turn down suffering of the past are an illustration of this, such as individuals who actually claim that the Holocaust never took place. Another example is people who believe that HIV doesn't hurt anyone and doesn't cause AIDS.[26] The second form of denial is to change how we frame the problem. An especially striking recent instance of this was the textbook company in Texas that described enslaved Africans in America as "workers," rather than as slaves.[27] Finally, the third type of denial is to reject the consequences of the problem.[28] For example, Giles may readily acknowledge the awfulness of human starvation but deny that he should pledge money to remedy the problem, saying, "What's the point? A little money isn't going to fix that!"

Sometimes we evade suffering because it throws us off balance and leaves us feeling just a little too exposed for our liking.

Remember our acute need to feel like we're in charge of our own fate, and how unsettling it is to realize that misfortune can strike at any moment? When we see other people battle hardships that happen to them through no fault of their own, it pulls us nearer to the plain truth that this could be our fate too. To guard ourselves against this disquieting reality, we step away from others' suffering. Unfortunately, as a 2015 study revealed, when we're in this disconnected mind-set, we're more apt to blame others for their hardship and are less inclined to help. More specifically, the study showed that when we get emotionally close to someone's story of suffering, like the feelings and thoughts of someone who experienced intimate partner violence, we're more prone to blame them and are less interested in helping them when we hear their story in the first person ("I"), as opposed to a more removed third person ("he" or she") account.[29]

Sidestepping Animal Suffering

Admittedly, the term *animal suffering* is misleading considering that we're animals too! But we certainly like to pretend we're not, don't we? We grant ourselves inner worlds that we oftentimes deny to our nonhuman friends. There are exceptions, of course. How many times have you or other people bestowed mental and emotional lives on pets, complete with feelings, thoughts, intentions, and a personality? For example, when our dog was alive, my husband, Guille, and I laughed about how Romeo loved me but didn't seem to respect my authority a whole lot. And we describe our parrot, Edgar, as being hot-tempered.

But, when it comes to the animals we consume for food, that's where we draw the line. And why? Well, we don't care for the notion of killing and eating living beings that we attribute thoughts and feelings to. We empathize with those animals and can picture the horror they'd experience as they're killed. We would certainly feel overwhelming terror if aliens came along with an appetite for humans and slaughtered us. But then, if we truly granted inner worlds to pigs, cows, ducks, chickens, and turkeys, to name a few, then pork, steak, burgers, and so on would be off the menu in a minute. Some cultures consider it perfectly appropriate to eat dogs. But in the United States and in other Western nations, dogs are "man's (and woman's) best friend," right? The idea of eating a dog here is not only unthinkable, it's literally a crime. Yet the systematic slaughter of pigs happens every day, and most people don't think about it.

For sure, this doesn't mean that those of us who eat animals are cruel, heartless monsters. Quite the opposite! Some serious mental twists are in order for people to continue eating the meat they enjoy and fitting in with their fellow omnivores, rather than going vegetarian or vegan. Specifically, people think of animals they view as food as having less of an inner world. This enables them to continue eating meat without thinking they're hurting a fully sentient being. In fact, when people reflect on the agony that animals endure in the meat industry, or when they anticipate eating meat in the near future, they're less apt to see the animals they eat as having mental and emotional lives.[30]

Shaking Off the Environment

Although more people are thinking about the environment now than they were back in 1965, by and large, we still have a tendency to turn down the dial on our alarm about the future of our planet. And why do we do that, especially when the Earth is the only home we have? Well, research suggests that this partly links back to our need to believe that we can control our fate and that we live in a fair world that won't harm us, at least as long as we're decent people. We seem to keep returning to that theme and with good reason. It reflects a forceful need within us. In point of fact, the more we believe in a controlled, fair universe, the more likely we are to be skeptical of environmental hazards. Even when researchers merely evoke ideas of a fair universe within us, we're less inclined to help the environment. But let's go back. Why would the idea of an even-handed world hamper our ability to face environmental concerns in the first place? One possibility is that the potentially disastrous results of human-made environmental problems like climate change go against our image of an orderly, controlled world. So, to keep hold of this belief and cushion ourselves against the angst of losing it, we turn down the dial on our concerns about the environment instead.[31] Another potential reason why we turn down the environmental dial is that we're trying to evade the policy ramifications that could come from admitting there's an issue. If we don't want to pursue the solutions, we probably won't want to pursue the problem.[32]

We have ways of rebuffing environmental warnings too. First, we can downplay the notion that environmental changes will yield drastic problems for people, animals, or the Earth in general. Second, we can dismiss the idea that everyone merits consideration when it comes to environmental concerns. For instance, we may disregard the needs of animals in the wild, elevating human concerns over theirs. Third, we can turn away from the idea that environmental concerns have anything to do with us, putting it off instead as other people's problem.[33]

Turning Up the Dial on Compassion

The world is a wondrous place, but let's face it, it's also rife with torment and overwhelming challenges. It would be too much to go through our daily lives totally attuned to it all 24/7, so it can be quite protective and adaptive for us to turn down the dial on it at times. All the same, we don't want to be so insulated that we lose touch with adversity or disregard places where we can make a difference. One way we can be more mindful and compassionate is to try meditation.

In a 2015 study, researchers trained people in a set of meditation techniques called "the four immeasurables":

- The first technique is a loving-kindness meditation, which essentially involves reflecting on your hopes for others as a way of engendering kindheartedness and lessening hostility.

- The second one is a compassion meditation, in which you think about and emotionally connect with others' hurt and then focus on your desire for others' distress to end. The purpose of this technique is also to build compassion and relax our tendency to cushion ourselves from others' suffering.
- The third practice is called an empathic joy meditation, which involves attending to something beneficial that's happening for someone else with the goal of letting go of jealousy.
- Finally, the fourth technique is known as an equanimity meditation. It's a peace and tranquility meditation in which you reflect on the similarity between yourself and others, and extend hopes of well-being to everyone. The purpose of this practice is to promote connectedness, and counter narrow-mindedness and bias about others.

After people practiced these techniques for three months, they showed greater signs of compassion along with fewer indicators that they were turning down the dial on others' pain. Presumably, you can apply these techniques toward humans or nonhuman animals, and although they stem from Buddhism, you certainly don't have to be Buddhist to practice them.[34] If you're interested in learning more, you'll find information in the Resources section at the end of this book.

To recap, we just journeyed through our tendency to turn down the dial on widespread problems, namely climate change and the suffering of human and nonhuman animals. Next, we'll examine one of the most potent kinds of denial of all—the denial of equality.

SHUTTING OUT

We're now going to explore how the *isms* sabotage us all. If you're realizing that you're in the dark when it comes to the powerful influence isms wield over your life and the lives of others, that's OK. Depending on what groups you're a part of, the extent and force of some isms may be easier to recognize than others. The ones that subject you to negative treatment, barriers to opportunity, or both can be more likely to stand out to you, while those that don't, including isms that place you in a position of advantage and privilege relative to others, can remain cloaked in dimness. Thankfully, we can start to shine a light on the spaces we don't see. Two people helped me discover this firsthand.

> *I was sixteen years old at the time of the Los Angeles riots. Despite the fact that some of the tumult was spreading to nearby Pasadena, I nonetheless visited a store there, undaunted. As I was walking back toward my car, two Black men pulled up in a truck. They looked furious and were yelling in my general direction.* Uh oh, somebody's in trouble! *I thought, glancing around to see whom they were so upset with. When I realized I was the only one on the entire block, I got the picture that they were hollering at me. Then they drove off. In light of the heightened racial tensions at the time, I attributed their reaction to my race and thought indignantly,* they shouldn't be yelling at me. I can't control my skin color! I didn't ask to be born White! *And then, a revelation dawned on my completely clueless self. As a White person, I never had to experience what it was like for someone to judge me because of my skin color. I got a flashing glimpse, a mere speck of sand, of what it's like to be on the receiving end of racism. It felt arbitrary and appalling, and it just lasted for a few seconds. Then the offense I felt on my own behalf quickly faded away. In its place came a surge of indignation on behalf of people from diverse racial backgrounds who had to face racism on a regular basis. I also*

felt embarrassed for being White, a group with a history of racial prejudice and privilege. I silently thanked those two men for helping me see what had been, admittedly, totally invisible to me a few moments before—the luxury I have, denied to many others, of not having to worry about whether anyone would treat me differently because of my skin color. They gave me one of the most valuable lessons of my life.

In our society there are a host of isms—racism, sexism, ageism, heterosexism, body-weight bias—I could go on. And even as the prejudice and discrimination that make up the isms target different groups of people, what they all share in common is that they deny people who are in minority groups—groups with less power or that are socially stigmatized—full equality and consideration. On top of that, as a society, we turn the dial down on the isms themselves by acting as if they aren't a reality or are a thing of the past. This is disastrous and ultimately self-defeating, because not only do the isms hurt society, they wound us as individuals too, regardless of whether we're on the receiving or the giving end of them. For instance, if we're in a disempowered group (e.g., Latinas), we're on guard for others' prejudice to undermine us, and if we're in a majority or empowered group (e.g., White men), we're watchful that others will assume we're prejudiced.[35] What's more, because isms deny equal opportunity, they go against the value of equality that we cherish in a number of societies.[36] It's lose-lose.

Arguably, equal opportunity is such a common societal value in our culture that many of us are tempted to claim that we don't really have any prejudices. Well, if you can say that you don't hold any unfavorable assumptions or attitudes, even unconsciously, about anyone—not prejudices based on their gender, gender identity, race, age, sexual orientation, body weight, physical ability, education level, financial status, career, political beliefs, religious beliefs, region of the country where they live, mental health, physical health, history of alcohol or substance abuse, or marital or family background—then you might be able to say you're immune to prejudice. But considering that it's a stretch, at best, to imagine that anyone can honestly say that, you're probably like every other human in the world and are not entirely bias free. That's OK. The goal is not to vilify but to focus on recognizing and questioning isms, for other people's benefit and for our own. When we dismiss the notion that we carry at least a kernel of bias within us, we entrench it even deeper. Only in the broad light of day can we sap its power.[37] On that note, let's explore a sample of the isms.

Racism

Arguably, racism and efforts to deny it are prevalent in society. Why do people downplay the reality of racism? There are multiple reasons. One element linked to the denial of racism is that people who are White are less likely to know about examples of racism in history, which is linked to a tendency to be less aware of instances of racism in the present.[38] Another reason why people deny racism is that they don't want to acknowledge the reality of their White privilege and power. If they did so, they'd face the unsettling question of whether all of their successes in life were fully earned through their own merit, or were influenced, at least in part, by the color of their skin. Some people also deny racism to hold onto the status quo and the social advantages they have, rather than relinquish some of their power. On the flip side, there are arguably those who don't want to face White privilege because it feels uncomfortable, upsetting, or embarrassing to unfairly and arbitrarily benefit at the expense of others. Another factor connected to this denial is that people may only picture racism in its more obvious, unconcealed forms—like the open use of racial slurs—rather than in its veiled forms, such as deliberately staying away from people of other races. And then there are also White people who try not to see race or discuss it, as if acknowledging it translates into being racist.[39] Yet, even when efforts to reduce racial awareness come from a well-intentioned place, they don't work. If anything, they're linked to prejudice, strain, and apprehension. In other words, what we don't want.[40]

And of course, racism itself is associated with a lot of other things that we don't want. For instance, the stress of racism has been shown to be related to family conflict.[41] What's more, racism threatens our lives—literally. White and Black people are at greater risk of dying when they live in more racist neighborhoods, regardless of the quality of those neighborhoods. What's more, they're prone to an early death if they live in neighborhoods with less racial bias but are racist themselves.[42] On top of all that, racism undermines our ability to live in a fair, inclusive, harmonious society, free from injustice in work performance reviews and criminal sentencing.[43]

Sexism

Another ism that often flies under our radar is sexism. One type of sexism is known as *hostile sexism,* which refers to feelings of animosity toward women who challenge old gender norms and, in so doing, are viewed as trying to strip men of their control and influence. The twin of this brand of sexism is *benevolent sexism,* which involves care and warmth toward women who adhere to old gender norms and don't change the status quo.[44] And even though benevolent sexism, like hostile sexism, maintains an imbalance of power, many men and women gravitate toward it.[45] Why? Because it offers apparent plus sides that a number of women say they value, such as receiving assistance, getting chivalrous treatment, being "wined and dined," and facing less intense career expectations.[46]

Yet, despite its appeal for many people, women and men both lose. For one, it hinders women's success in the workplace, eating away at family earnings. As of this writing, for every dollar a man makes, a woman makes roughly seventy-nine cents, and indirect workplace discrimination and underestimation of women's abilities and leadership capacity are rampant.[47] What's more, gender roles at home inadvertently impact gender bias at work, as men married to women who stay at home are more likely to disapprove of women in the workforce and to deny them promotions. And when men marry women who don't work, their support for women in the workplace takes a dip.[48]

Sexism also undermines relationships. Women and men who agree with the tenets of benevolent sexism are more inclined to leave their partners if they don't fulfill their ideal standards of affection and tenderness.[49] What's more, our beliefs about gender equality are wildly out of step with our views on dating. According to a 2015 poll, 78 percent of men and women believe in total gender equality.[50] Yet, a 2014 survey reveals that 82 percent of men and 73 percent of women expect the man to foot the bill for the first date, a belief that reflects benevolent sexism.[51]

Heterosexism

This is another ism with a far-reaching history of open approval, continuing to this day.[52] But make no mistake, heterosexism isn't a gay, lesbian, or bisexual issue. It's a human issue; one that damages the lives of people who are its targets and eats away at everyone's ability to live in a secure and just society. True, same-sex marriage is now legal across the United States, which affords a greater measure of justice, but this happened only recently. What's more, there are currently no laws at the federal level that prohibit heterosexist discrimination in every workplace. Of course, many organizations implement their own antidiscrimination policies, including roughly 87 percent of the Fortune 500. Sadly, this doesn't help the over 40 percent of people who have faced heterosexist discrimination at their job.[53] In addition to prejudice and discrimination, aggression against sexual minorities is all too frequent, with nearly 50 percent of people who identify as gay, lesbian, or bisexual facing verbal abuse, and around 20 percent being the victims of violence, of a crime against their property, or both.[54] And when alcohol goes in the mix, it gets even more volatile, as people who hold heterosexist attitudes are more likely to harm another person when they're under the influence. For instance, findings from 2015 studies offer evidence that the more heterosexual men follow gender norms of masculinity and hold heterosexist attitudes, the more combative they are against gay men when they've been drinking.[55]

Weight Bias

A prejudicial attitude against people because of their weight is another potent bias that oftentimes goes undetected or is blatantly condoned. Sadly, people who are obese face rampant weight-related social stigma and prejudice, which are linked to having an eating disorder, distress and unease, and staying away from other people or pursuits.[56] And not only does weight bias harm individuals who are obese, it hurts everyone by drawing strict boundaries around what is considered an acceptable versus an unacceptable body and diminishing our value of social fairness. For instance, one remarkable study revealed that people who see a biased picture of an obese couple eating snacks are more likely to be in favor of denying them fertility treatments compared to people who see an unbiased image of an obese couple hand in hand.[57]

Ageism

Last but not least, we come to another widespread ism, and the only one that we will all face, provided we live long enough. To be sure, ageism targets younger people too, but given the harm of ageism toward older adults, we'll focus our attention there. And unfortunately, it has immensely powerful consequences. For one, older individuals are all too aware of unfavorable stereotypes about people who are older, and many dread the thought of confirming these notions. In fact, when older people are attuned to negative aging stereotypes, they're more likely to perform worse on a test of cognitive ability. And why? Presumably, they were so nervous they'd confirm the stereotype of an older person with cognitive issues that they couldn't focus on the task. It's a well-known phenomenon known as stereotype threat. It happens when our nervousness that we'll fit a stereotype lessens our performance and leads us to, paradoxically, match the stereotype we're trying to avoid.[58] What's more, unfavorable aging stereotypes and worries about aging seem be a part of what drives some older people's memory concerns, beyond any actual memory changes they may be experiencing.[59] So, as a society, not only do older people lose when it comes to age-related bias, younger people do too. After all, one day the young will be old.

EATING AWAY AT ISMS

Now, as we approach the end this stop, let's look at ways we can fight against the isms, for ourselves, others, and our society.

Contact

Arguably, some of the strongest research points to a beautiful way of reducing the isms: constructive, kindly contact with diverse groups of people. This predicts diminished ageism among younger people toward older individuals,[60] reduces racism,[61] lessens heterosexism,[62] and alleviates body weight prejudice.[63] In fact, contact is such a helpful force that it can even lessen prejudice when people simply imagine having contact with someone else,[64] or when they read favorable stories in the media that go against unfavorable stereotypes.[65] This was probably a big factor in the radical progress within just the last few years for equal rights for gay, lesbian, and bisexual (GLB) people. Although we still have an incredibly long way to go as a society, the normalization of people who identify as GLB in the popular media is likely to have encouraged more people to come out, making it possible for many heterosexuals who may have previously been prejudiced to have a positive experience with a GLB person socially, at work, and within their extended family. Sadly, transgender people also face far-reaching prejudice and discrimination, and a significant number of media portrayals of transgender people are unfavorable. Hopefully, we'll soon see a substantial shift for the better in how frequently and positively transgender people are represented, as the media could be a potent force for improvement.[66]

Education

Another strategy that science supports is education, particularly with regard to sexism. Considering that many men and women are in plenty of contact, more contact is unlikely to be useful. But information on the harmful realities of sexism is another story. When men and women receive education on benevolent sexism, and how socially widespread and damaging it is, they're much less likely to favor it.[67]

Willingness to Try, Stumble, and Try Again

Believe it or not, another way to combat isms is the simple desire to live as unprejudiced a life as possible. Research suggests that when we're driven to be unbiased, we're more likely to be upset when we falter. And it's that drive to be unbiased plus the experience of stumbling as we try that predicts a greater learning experience. We're more likely to be unbiased the next time around than if we never made a misstep at all.[68]

To sum up this stop, we delved into three main ways that we turn the dial down at the level of society. First, we saw how people have far more influence on us than we'd like to think. Second, we examined our tendency to cocoon ourselves from suffering and other daunting, large-scale issues. And third, we looked at how we deny equal consideration to others through isms as well as denial of the isms themselves. Before we officially leave this stop, let's proceed to exercises that will help you apply what we've explored here in your social world.

EXERCISES

Exercise 1: Going with the Flow

This exercise is intended to help you to know when following people's influence is good for you, and to cultivate compassion for problems and suffering when aloofness pulls you astray. For this exercise, you'll want a separate sheet, paper or digital.

1. For the next week, please observe and jot down moments when you experience the pull of social influence, regardless of whether you go along with it. Make a note of whether this is an influence you'd like to follow or not, and why. Then over the next week, try to follow at least one positive influence you noticed, writing down what you did and how it felt.
2. Notice a moment when you feel detached from a widespread problem or suffering. First, rate on a 0 to 10 scale how much empathy you feel (0 is none, and 10 is the most you could possibly feel). Next, see if you can heighten your empathy by trying to picture yourself in that position, or remember a time when you faced something even remotely similar. Now, recheck yourself on that same scale to see if you notice a difference. It's OK if you don't. The key is simply to be aware and to practice tuning in.

Exercise 2: Confronting Isms

On this stop, we explored isms and how they hurt us all. In this exercise, you'll have a chance to spot and challenge the isms in your life. For this exercise, you'll also want to use a separate sheet.

1. Arguably, virtually all of us belong to at least one minority group that is the target of unfavorable bias, and many of us come from at least one majority group that has privileges.
   - Please write down all of the social groups you belong to, such as those identified with your race, your gender, your gender identity, your sexual orientation, your age, your education, your socioeconomic status, where you live, your body type, and so on. For each group you listed, think about whether it is a majority or minority group.

- Next, please jot down five unfavorable beliefs you have about yourself because of your membership in any of these groups. Challenge yourself to reframe these beliefs, and see if you can spot counterexamples in the media, in daily life, in your past, or in yourself.
- Finally, reflect on any groups that you have unfavorable attitudes and beliefs toward, no matter how minor, and write down three. Examples could be based on race, gender, gender identity, age, political party, religious affiliation, sexual orientation, financial or educational background, body type, dietary habits, personal style, or family background, etc. If you can't think of any, that's OK. Try paying attention to your reactions (e.g., thoughts, feelings, behavior) over the course of the next several days and notice if you have any that might offer you a clue to negative biases you hold.
- After you've got your list, challenge yourself by writing down why you might have these particular biases, and by reflecting on how they could be incorrect. Next, make a commitment over the next month to expose yourself to positive information and experiences that counter at least one bias. At the end of the month, go back and reflect on whether your bias has shifted and if you've noticed a difference in how you feel.

7

DENIAL AT THE LEVEL OF LIFE AND DEATH

The irony of a man's condition is that the deepest need is to be free of the anxiety of death and annihilation; but it is life itself which awakens it, and so we must shrink from being fully alive.

—Ernest Becker, *The Denial of Death*

Death can take us at any moment. This is a reality that we understand at an abstract level, but not one that we *really* sit with, if you know what I mean. Most of us have probably heard the cliché "live every day like it's your last," but most of us don't wake up *truly* thinking "this could be the last time my head rests on a pillow. I may not live through the day and make it back to my home and my loved ones. And even if I do, any one of my loved ones might not survive this day." We tend to assume death will happen someday, but surely not today, or next week, or a year from now. Perhaps that's true. Still, for almost all of us, we have the shared fate of living day to day not knowing exactly when and how we're going to die. And this uncertainty, coupled with the knowledge that Death could, quite literally, come for us at any second, can be a terrifying, deeply disturbing reality to live with.

So we crank the dial way down on the Grim Reaper's random timing, along with our awareness that our demise and the end of everything we cherish are inescapable. We don't actually walk around in our daily lives looking at the trees, driving in our cars, walking through our offices, spending times with our friends and our partner fully realizing that all of this is going to end someday. Like Wesley in the following example, many of us get caught up in the whirlwind of life, forgetting to appreciate all of the people, pets, places, and moments that we love and will eventually lose.

> Oh no, I'm late! *Wesley panics. His alarm didn't go off. Surging adrenaline flashes him from a foggy haze to crisp alertness.* At this rate, I'm looking at walking into our client meeting thirty minutes late! It'll be a miracle if Dave doesn't fire me! *Wesley fumbles frantically with his tie. Later, he wonders if hearing "you're fired!" might have been better than the actual consequences. Simpler, anyway.*
>
> *"Wes!" his boss rants, pacing wildly in his office. "Do you have any idea how unprofessional we look when the lead member of our sales team waltzes into the meeting thirty minutes late?"*
>
> *"I'm really sorry, Dave," Wesley stammers as his eyes fall toward the floor. "I don't know how it happened. My alarm just didn't go off."*
>
> *"You know what, Wes?" Dave says, stopping to eye him squarely, "I don't care if God himself flicked off your alarm! You get in here on time! We lost that client, and it's all because of you! Now get the hell out of my office before I say anything I'll regret."*
>
> *Wesley keeps his composure until he makes it back to his car at the day's end. Then, to his shock, he breaks down. "Christ, I hate my life!" he blurts. "I make less than most of my friends at this meaningless corporate sludge job and just have a lonely apartment to come home to. And I'm forty-three years old, so it's even more downhill from here! Wonderful!" He sobs out every loss and disappointment he's been carrying. A pent-up dam bursts at last.*
>
> *As the waters dry, he brings himself back to the here and now.* Well, thankfully it's Friday, and I've got the weekend to

> recover, so what now? *he thinks, laughing in surprise at the well of feeling that burst out of him.* I think some nice Thai takeout and a comedy are in order. Oh crap, I'm almost out of gas. Better take care of that first. *He drives to a nearby station and fills the tank, then goes inside to treat himself to a candy bar. A minute later, a gunman bursts in, shooting the cashier and taking all of the money in the register. Wesley crouches down in one of the aisles, horrified and shaking. But the gunman knows he is there. Blinded with terror, Wesley pleads for his life. The cares that had weighed so heavily shrink to nothing. And the life that seemed so bleak an hour before emerges a shining, precious treasure. Now he is desperate for the gift of growing older. His loving family, his loyal friends, the nice apartment waiting for him, all the laughter, those warm sunrises—these images stay with him as the gunman hits him across his forehead with his gun and Wesley sinks unconscious to the floor.*

As Wesley found himself doing, we can get so caught up in the headaches and hassles that we lose sight of the fact that these are temporary problems and perhaps not as important as they appear in the bright spotlight of facing death.

This brings us to the final stop on our tour. Here we're going to explore our efforts to turn the dial down on the reality that we're mortal and life is limited. This stop will involve three primary parts. First, we'll look at how a number of us despise the idea of aging, just as Wesley did. Second, we'll examine how we protect ourselves against the reality of our death, and the benefits and problems of doing so. Third, we'll delve into the paradoxical truth that even as the awareness of death can be overpowering, it can be profoundly life giving, offering us the opportunity to live with more abundance, enjoyment, and gratitude—as we hope that Wesley was able to do. At the end of this stop, you'll be able to try some exercises that will help you to re-evaluate your views on aging, to explore how you cope with death, and to use the reality of death to bring brighter meaningfulness to life.

FORGET THE BIRTHDAY PRESENTS! HOW ABOUT NO MORE BIRTHDAYS?

Our societal attitudes toward growing older are utterly fascinating. We place youth up on a pedestal and push aging down in the dust, shuddering with each advancing year. In effect, we're dancing a self-defeating tango, stepping on our own toes by yearning for a time that we can never return to and loathing the years that will surely come, assuming we don't die before we get there. The end result of that way of thinking is that our best years are eternally behind us, and the worst is always yet to come. Ugh! What a horrible way to live! Yet many of us live in this way. We seem to box youth into such a confined, worshipful space, and then we brace ourselves once we age beyond that box with each birthday, cringing as we refer to ourselves as old. I remember being twenty-seven and feeling surprised to hear someone refer to himself in a depressing tone as old when he was just thirty-two! Since that day, I've heard people ranging in age from their early twenties to their eighties refer to themselves as old. Youth seems to have an early expiration date, indeed.

And no wonder we long to prevent Father Time from paying us our annual visit. Many people of all ages hold exceedingly negative, not to mention inaccurate, stereotypes about aging. I hear it all the time, in conversations with friends and colleagues, and in all the media. An aversion to getting older is common across many cultures. One study that pulled together findings on cultural mind-sets toward older individuals across twenty-three nations is a fitting illustration. Even though attitudes toward aging appeared to differ across countries to some degree, there were biases that most shared. The notion that people lose their physical appeal and overall capability as they get older was pervasive, as was the idea that society holds people in a less favorable light as they age.[1]

Arguably, another immensely potent stereotype is that older individuals are relatively unhappy, past their prime and the joyful, happy-go-lucky days of the past.[2] Whether we're in our early thirties or our late sixties, we can't seem to kick the idea that people are going to feel less cheerfulness and enjoyment as they age, even when we've witnessed ourselves feeling more joyful over time up to that point. What's more, the idea isn't true! Psychological research suggests that, on balance, our spirits are likely to rise, with our contentment either going up or at least remaining the same and our distress going down.[3] For instance, a study looking at people age eighteen to ninety-four found no link between age and happy feelings, suggesting that people feel upbeat just as often and as powerfully later in their life as in their youth. On the flip side, from age eighteen to age sixty, there's a constant *downturn* in how often people have upsetting feelings. And even though distress begins to rise from age sixty-five to ninety-four, the change was insignificant and didn't remotely creep up to how often people age eighteen to thirty-four feel upset.[4]

In other words, when we consider the balance of steady pleasant emotions and declining distress over time, people are actually likely to feel more content from age sixty onward than they are between their late teens and mid-thirties! So if we're silently cursing our next birthday, grimacing and cringing as we imagine our days of joy fading ever further behind us in life's rearview mirror, perhaps we need to take a fresh approach to this whole aging business. In fact, here's an invitation to us all. For our next birthday, let's reflect, rejoice, and make the most of it!

Now of course, aging itself is not an automatic potion of happiness. The key is to live and age well, but then this is true at all points of life. And part of aging well is to live a healthy lifestyle to maintain physical wellness over time. But what does health have to do with happiness? A great deal, according to one study showing that when people age fifty and over view their physical well-being as unsatisfactory, their chances of being miserable are virtually threefold.[5]

But another part of successful aging is up in our heads, in how we think. For instance, feeling older than one's true age has been found to forecast less contentment with life for people with a negative outlook on aging, but not for people with an optimistic view.[6] And there are other ways that aging attitudes and stereotypes can affect us. For one, regardless of our age, we may allow unfavorable stereotypes about aging to encourage us to create as much separation as possible between us and old—for example, getting cosmetic surgery, viewing older people as different from us, and supporting negative stereotypes ourselves.[7] These stereotypes apparently can affect our hearing too. One study showed that when we hold gloomy attitudes about aging and about our looks, we do more poorly on a hearing test three years later regardless of other factors that can affect hearing loss or how we were hearing before. To give you an idea of what this means, the degree of hearing loss was roughly in line with what people would normally experience over eight years![8]

So far, we've been talking about conscious stereotypes. Let's go below the surface of our awareness for a moment. As we go about life, we're exposed to a ton of information, and although a good deal of it reaches us consciously, a lot of it affects us unconsciously too. And societal stereotypes about aging are no exception. They can even impact our abilities when we don't consciously realize it. For instance, when people unconsciously encounter favorable and unfavorable aging stereotypes related to mental and physical abilities, incredibly, this impacts what people can do on mental and physical tests. Those who get exposed to good stereotypes about aging and physical ability do best on a physical test, whereas those who encounter bad physical stereotypes do the worst. Likewise, people who unconsciously receive unfavorable mental stereotypes about aging struggle most on a cognitive ability test, and those who are exposed to beneficial stereotypes perform best.[9]

The results of a 2014 study with people age sixty and over are especially dramatic. People unconsciously encountered uplifting stereotypes about aging over the course of four weeks. Not only did the unconscious treatment boost people's stereotypes about aging, but it also brightened how they viewed their own aging and improved physical abilities, such as how strong they were, how well they could balance, and how fast they could walk. Incredibly, it had a greater impact on people's physical abilities than an exercise program that lasted for six months![10]

As we leave the realm of the unconscious and come back up to the level of our conscious awareness, we come upon another surprising fact. Our assumptions about aging can, ironically, play a role in preventing us from taking a crucial step that will help us age well—exercise. Among a group of people age twenty-six to ninety-five, it was shown that one of the blockades connected with being physically active is the assumption that any unwelcome differences people notice in their physique, such as how strong they are or how much vigor they feel, must be due to getting older. This makes sense if we stop and think about it. After all, if we presume that our body is the way it is because of how old we are rather than our inactive lifestyle, we might assume such differences are an inevitable part of aging and not think to do anything about it. Indeed, the people in this group who were inactive and traced unwanted body changes to their age were also more inclined to say that exercise is less important as people get older.[11] But on the flip side, enhanced attitudes about aging among people over age sixty-five are linked to more physical activity.[12]

And exercise is *pivotal* to successful aging—I can't shout that loudly enough. The thing is, we don't even have to put in a whole lot of effort to reap a whopping payoff. Consider Alzheimer's disease, for instance. Whenever I talk with groups of people about lifestyle and aging, and I ask who's concerned that they'll develop Alzheimer's disease or another form of dementia, virtually every single person raises their hand. It's easy to believe that this is an inherent part of aging for many of us and that there's nothing we can do, but there's research that tells us otherwise:

- People who exercise the equivalent of a 2.3-mile run or more each day (or about twenty-eight minutes per day if you're jogging twelve-minute miles) are roughly 40 percent less likely to die from Alzheimer's disease compared to someone who runs less than .66 miles a day (or about eight minutes if you're jogging at a twelve-minute-per-mile pace).

- On top of that, when we eat just three or more pieces of fruit each day, we're over 60 percent less likely to die of Alzheimer's disease.[13]

That's right, three pieces of fruit a day and a 2.3-mile jog (or an equal substitute if you can't run, or aren't a fan of it) most days of the week offer you powerful protection against Alzheimer's disease. Of course, it's not a guarantee that you won't develop the disease, but it massively improves your odds. Who doesn't want that?

So, on the whole, if you have a distaste for getting older, and you think that your attempts to turn down the dial on the reality of aging won't affect you, you might want to reconsider. Your own stereotypes toward aging, as well as the ones you encounter in society, whether you're conscious of them or not, may well be influencing how you feel and what you can do more than the number of candles on your birthday cake. Aging isn't a one-size-fits-all process. The attitudes we hold and the lifestyle we choose strongly impact our lives and well-being as we get older, which is excellent news. Unlike the passage of time, these are two things we actually can control!

All the same, we can have the most shining perspective on aging in the world and be beacons of healthy living, but we're still inevitably going to die sooner or later. That is something we have zero control over, and many of us have a tough time facing that. So we do our best to turn down the dial on this certainty. On the one hand, this winds up giving us more of what we don't want, but on the other, it allows us to continue living our lives without becoming paralyzed by obsessing about our mortality. As we come to the second leg of our stop, we'll turn here.

DITCHING DEATH

It's insanely mind-blowing to know—and I mean to *really* know—that we're going to die. The concept is so daunting and massive that it's almost impossible to wrap our minds around it. And permitting ourselves to fully settle into that certainty—as much as we can, anyway—can be anxiety provoking at best and, for many of us, grim, terrifying, and heartbreaking. But most of the time we don't let that happen, moseying though life without devoting much thought to the solemn reality that, at one time or another, everything we love and care about and the countless things we take for granted—all of it—will come to an end. And thank goodness we can, for the most part, turn the dial down on that reality. Can you imagine constantly walking around with the full-blown awareness glaring you right in the face that you will unquestionably cease to exist, along with everything that matters to you? It would be awful. It would probably be challenging to function day to day with peace of mind. Weightiness, anxiety, and sadness would likely shade moments ordinarily filled with lightness, serenity, and joy. Once I gave a talk about this general topic, and someone came up to me after everyone else left, sobbing. This reality hit her, an absolute truth that she never actually considered. It's not that she didn't intellectually understand that everyone dies. Surely, she knew this. No, what happened is that she really got it on an emotional level. And that is altogether different. I understood, feeling for her and with her on a profoundly human level. We are, in the end, all in it together.

So what do we do with it, together? Well, one influential, well-researched perspective is that we try to turn the dial down on our inescapable advance toward death by trying to attain a sense of deathlessness, of immortality. But how do we do that?

It depends on how central death is in our awareness. Let's start with thoughts of death that are a little more removed from our minds but ready to pop up. For example, imagine that a TV program with someone grieving prompts you to contemplate the end of your own life. Then a friend calls and tells you something funny. The conversation diverts your attention away so that these thoughts are still lingering in the background but are no longer at the forefront of your mind. How do we respond to death when it's sitting just in the shadows of our attention?

In that case, we're more likely to go along with our culture's ideals, customs, institutions, practices, ways of thinking, and standards of behavior. Why would this comfort us? For one, when we stand united with our culture, which will live on after our death, we can feel like we live on too through this grander whole. Second, when we live in keeping with our culture's values, we feel better about ourselves, a soothing feeling that helps us ease our distress about dying. So essentially, our connection to culture and approval of ourselves both turn down the dial on our death.

So far, we've been talking about how we handle death in the back of our mind. But what if the topic of our own death is right at the forefront of our thoughts? Then, rather than following our culture, we tend to take other approaches, such as aiming our attention somewhere else so we don't have to think about death, or magnifying our bill of health to feel less vulnerable.[14] Ultimately, regardless of whether our mortality is in the front or the back of our minds, we have ways of dialing it down. Let's explore some of these.

Turning Away

One reaction is to push death away. For instance, how nervous we consciously feel about dying is related to how much we unconsciously reject the notion of our own death. And our unconscious refusal to accept death is also connected to less of a desire to make preparations for it.[15] Strikingly, we seem to be so compelled to evade death that when we reflect on the end of our life, we'll even try to escape death by minimizing how similar we are to someone with an incurable type of cancer.[16] But we can turn away from death in a subtler way. For instance, one study suggests that we're driven to use work as a shield against our mortality. Specifically, when we think about our demise, we're more inclined to want to work, and when we imagine that we're going to be able to start working at a job we desire, thoughts of our death pop up less readily. And what about when we picture stumbling blocks to being able to work? Then, thoughts of our death are more likely to enter the picture.[17]

Connected to Something Greater and to Ourselves

We touched on how we turn down the dial on our death by identifying with culturally supported ideals, institutions, and practices and having an encouraging, positive view of ourselves. But let's go into more detail on how we do this. For instance, research has shown that some people's allegiance to their country can be strong enough to mitigate the effect that thoughts of their own death have on them.[18]

Even mere symbols of our culture can buffer us from the fright of our death. People can identify with a particular style of music, such as heavy metal or reggae, as an expression of their subculture so that it becomes a way to ease their disquiet about death.[19]

Furthermore, we can seek an everlasting shield against death by believing in eternal life, which most cultures value in some form.[20] For instance, some cultures regard their ancestors with veneration, such as China and many Southeast Asian countries, where a kind of immortality of past generations is a part of their belief systems. Of course, many of us find comfort in our religious beliefs, especially when there is promise of an afterlife. However, there can also be a great fear of death among those whose religions teach that there is not only a heaven for those who adhere to their doctrines, but also a hell, or a similar realm of eternal punishment, for those who fail to meet certain standards of belief and behavior.

Finally, on another personal level, we can reach toward deathlessness through procreation. Thoughts of death spur people to value having a larger family,[21] and people across cultures see themselves living on through their children and the generations that will follow.

And what about how we treat ourselves? When we face reminders of our demise, we can actually be more inclined to make positive lifestyle changes that might extend our lives.[22] In a similar vein, when thoughts of death are at the front of our mind, we are likely to respond by saying that we're going to care for ourselves better. But what happens when those thoughts fade into the background? Then we actually may have less resolve to nurture our health! It's possible that we would then turn down the dial on our eventual demise by turning to other ideals and values that we cherish and that reflect who we are.[23]

Averting Our Animality

We know that our body is precisely what makes us mortal. So another way we strive to evade death is to shun our physical, animal self. For instance, when we're aware of our death, it's been found that we may turn down the dial on our connection to animals and feel greater revulsion toward what symbolizes our bodily being, namely animals, body fluids, and wastes.[24] And our motivation to push a wedge between us and our bodies can also impact how we react to sex. More specifically, when we're more mindful of our connection to animals, we tend to be less likely to feel attracted to the fleshly, bodily dimension of sex after thinking of our own death, even as the allure of the less animalistic and amorous elements of sex remain the same.[25]

All in all, we have a menu of options for turning down the dial on our mortality so we can get on with the business of living, rather than constantly carrying death alongside us. And in some cases, our ability to turn down the dial on our death is even more consequential than we imagine. For instance, what would happen if our awareness of death hit us when we couldn't seem to turn down the dial?

Picture someone who struggles to feel worthwhile. He hates his job and is deeply dissatisfied with how his life is going, a life that he doesn't view as purposeful or meaningful. Then one day, he finds himself reflecting on his existence and eventual death.

What effect do you think these thoughts would have on you if you were in this situation? It depends. If they're at the forefront of your mind, they're probably not going to have a powerful impact, because you can still turn down the dial by focusing on something else. For example, you could go for a run, watch a TV show, or simply turn your thoughts to a less disturbing topic.

The problematic part is what happens when our awareness of death sits in the back of our mind, where it can still affect us. If we have a low sense of self-worth, we're missing a significant way of turning down the dial on our fear of death. In this case, we would be more likely to have even less contentment with life, to have diminished vigor and sense of purpose, lower intellectual curiosity, greater nervousness, and less contact with other people.[26] We would be even more vulnerable when we are having a particularly hard time. Then it depends on what we think about afterward. If we happen to reflect on important failures in our past, then awareness of our death coupled with a life we're already displeased with can actually leave us more likely to want to die at an earlier age, a reflection of abandoned hope. On the other hand, remembering worthwhile goals that we successfully reached doesn't pull us farther down into the same somber place, even though we're displeased with our life and know that we can never escape dying.[27]

So truly, awareness of our death can have a strikingly dramatic impact, holding the potential to pull us down quite forcefully, even to the point that we want to live less. Not only do we need to be able to turn down the dial on death to live day to day, but that "down" dial can even help us remain engaged with life. In fact, we probably shouldn't spend much time reflecting upon the end of life until we're able to find some source of comfort in the face of death.

On the other hand, let's not paint awareness of death with broad brushstrokes and dismiss it as inherently problematic or bad. To be sure, it can be overpowering and terrifying to contemplate the end of our existence. At the same time, to live entirely in the dark of this somber truth deprives us of the priceless capacity to step back, behold the panorama of life, and grasp what truly matters. Awareness of death has a strange capacity to inspire and strengthen us too, and this is where we now turn.

THE END OF LIFE CAN BE LIFE GIVING

It's so easy to get caught up in the daily cares and hassles of life, isn't it? The high-pressure meeting that you've been fretting over at night. The tension in your neck that nags you in traffic all the way home from work. Little quirks in others that irk the daylights out of you. The dishwasher that broke. Your car's flat tire. Your child's stomach flu that's keeping you away from work. Oh, and then there are the insecurities that bubble up and nip at virtually every person from time to time, in some fashion or another. If you can identify with some or all of this, or if you've ever had a moment when you just sighed up to the sky, wondering when it will stop, I hear you. It's called being alive in what can, at times, be a crazy world. True, life brings profound loss and crisis to most of us sooner or later, but it surely delivers minor headaches, inconveniences, petty stresses, and hectic moments to nearly all of us with the regularity of the daily news.

But what's particularly fascinating about us humans is that, not only do we tend to heighten the weight of everyday stress, we have a habit of shrinking the importance of life's splendid gifts that surround us. Those hugs and kisses with your partner when you get home, belly laughs at your favorite comic, lunch with a good friend, constellations of stars on a clear night, an evening walk in early spring, a good deed for someone in need, taking a break with a steaming cup of tea or coffee, a meaningful conversation with a colleague, digging into a delightful book or movie, or the rustle of leaves on a fall afternoon. You get the idea. If we're not paying attention, we can allow the value of these simple but enchanting, heartening moments to pass. Perhaps we're so caught up in everyday hassles that these delightful experiences blur into a hazy background, kind of like what we'd see if we were on a speeding train and we peeked out the window. Or maybe we take these moments for granted and dismiss them as commonplace, in the process twisting our standard for what it takes to amuse, fascinate, and gratify us, so that only what's dramatic, uncommon, and unfamiliar wins our appreciation. Regardless of how we dim the lights on these bright spots in our days, the outcome is that we essentially suck the enchantment right out of life and let the inevitable strains and troubles define our days.

Mercifully, this does not have to be our fate. We can cut the daily cares that seem so urgent down to size. We have the ability to awaken to how extraordinary the people, scenes, activities, and moments in our daily life are. And ironically, a robust way for us to vitalize our lives is to turn toward rather than away from the idea of death. Just as our ability to deny death is crucial at times, an acute awareness of it can be pivotal at other times for us to live life on our own terms. You may be asking, "How can our awareness of death breathe brightness into my life?" Let's explore a couple of perspectives on this question.

One idea is that we need to be able to face the certainty of death directly to live life wholeheartedly. In other words, we need to be willing to face the deaths of people we love if we're going to open up our hearts to them, rather than hold a part of ourselves back to guard against being hurt. To experience the life we sincerely want, in our day-to-day lives we must leave ourselves open to the awareness that we and those we love will die. Although it's understandable to do otherwise—to shield our hearts from love and hide from peril—it's still a fruitless endeavor, as death is the endgame for us all.[28] Sure, we may be avoiding risks and intimacy in the belief that we're keeping ourselves safer and free from hurt, but then it's worth asking: Are we willing to stop truly living just to stave off pain and the inevitability of death? Are we open to paying the price of being lonely and loveless solely so our hearts never ache from loss?

Another view is that death elevates how much we cherish life precisely by allowing us to have only so much of it. Remember how we talked about the human tendency to prize the unusual and the uncommon in life? The same applies to life itself. For instance, coming across something in our environment that reminds us of death can motivate us to cherish life more highly.[29] Similarly, we can join those who, by envisioning their remaining years of life as being shorter, value the feeling of serenity more than if they imagine having plenty of years left to live.[30] What's more, thinking about our death can actually enhance our thankfulness for our life.[31] But regardless of how or why it happens, it's simply awe-inspiring that, in the dusk of death, there is the possibility for more enthusiasm for life.

To recap, we explored three realms on this stop of our tour. First, we walked through our tendency to turn down the dial on aging and the problems we face in doing so. Second, we went on to look at our efforts to turn down the dial on the overwhelming and frightening awareness of our death, and we noticed that such denial is a mixed bag. It gives us a hand in living day to day, yet it can also deliver more of what we don't want. Then we considered the flip side, the advantages in life that come to us when we're willing to turn toward the reality of our death, at least at times, rather than race from it. Now, as we prepare to bring the final stop of our tour to an end, let's proceed to exercises that will offer you the chance to bring what we've explored more fully into your life.

EXERCISES

Exercise 1: Friendship with Your Older Self

On this stop, we realized that when we embrace aging with a brighter attitude, aging returns the favor and embraces us, treating us with more kindness as the years roll by. This exercise is designed to help you challenge your views on aging so that you can grasp the process of getting older in a more spirited, optimistic fashion. In other words, here you'll have a chance to work for, rather than push against, your older self. For this exercise, you'll want a separate sheet, paper or digital.[32]

1. Imagine yourself as someone who is much older than you are now. Really try to envision what you'll be like, how you'll be living, and what you'll be doing. Importantly, don't write down the vision you hope for, but what you authentically believe. Does this vision match any aging stereotypes that you're aware of? Or is it different? Would your older self agree with these stereotypes, and how would your current self feel to be stereotyped in these ways? How would your older self like to be seen?

2. Now, picture your older self as you would like to be, regardless of whether it fits any stereotypes or flies directly in the face of them. Try to imagine in as much detail as you can the kind of person you really want to grow into. For instance, what will be your outlook on life? What does your lifestyle look like? Are you active? What are your eating habits? What kind of social, romantic, sexual, and leisure life do you have? Are you working, or have you put that behind you? Are you engaged in any other activities that mean a great deal to you? How do you feel about yourself? You could take this in any direction that's personally meaningful to you. Just focus on picturing the older you that you want to become!

3. We learned that we have far more control over the road we take as we age than we thought. So please write down five doable changes you're willing to start making now based upon your most desired older self. For instance, perhaps you want to be strong and energetic, but you're not exercising now, so you might start

by going for brisk walks ten minutes per day, three days per week. Maybe you want to be healthy and protect yourself against a range of diseases, and so you decide to add an extra piece of fruit a day to your diet. Or maybe you want to be financially comfortable, so you start saving a set amount that you can easily afford from your paycheck and put it into a retirement account through your bank. You might even take money that you would normally use on more frivolous expenses, like that expensive morning cup of coffee, and invest it in your older self instead!

Exercise 2: Facing Death

On this stop, we explored how our awareness of death can enrich our life, as well as how it can pull us downward in certain circumstances. If you are at a miserable place in your life, you feel badly about yourself and your ability to improve your life, or you don't feel hopeful as you look toward the future, please do not try this exercise now. Instead, skip directly to the epilogue and then consider looking through the Resources section for first steps you can take to start enhancing the quality of your life. Then, when you're feeling like you're in a better space, return to this exercise. Otherwise, please continue.

This exercise is a chance for you to take stock of how you cope with death and to draw on an awareness of death to forge greater meaning in your life. You'll also want to use a separate sheet.

1. Please think about moments when you became more aware of your own eventual death, even briefly. What kinds of feelings came up? How did you react? Was there anything you did or anything you told yourself that was helpful? What can you think of to tell yourself, or what have you heard others say about death, that resonates and could ease your fears when these thoughts arise? If you can't think of anything to say to comfort yourself, try seeking out ideas by searching for quotes on death and the end of life. For instance, a simple Google search led me to a wonderful example in this classic poem:[33]

Because I could not stop for Death –
He kindly stopped for me –
The Carriage held but just Ourselves –
And Immortality.

—Emily Dickinson, excerpt from
"Because I could not stop for Death"

2. Now, please take some time to turn your attention toward your eventual death. What feelings and thoughts arise? Do you notice yourself feeling more grateful? Please write down the twenty things you will miss the most. If more than twenty ideas come to mind, write more if you wish. Afterward, did you notice any problems, hassles, or insecurities that just don't seem as important? Has your perspective on life changed in any way? If so, how? Are there any changes you feel inspired to make in your life? If so, please list one change that you deeply want to start making, along with a specific, doable step you'll take to make it happen.

3. Considering that we need the ability to turn the dial down on death as well as up, when you're ready to ease the dial down a bit, please reflect on the following:

   - We're all part of a larger culture, as well as subcultures. Please jot down twenty viewpoints, activities, and practices that your culture prizes and that you also highly value and why. For instance, perhaps it's important to you to be kind to others, or maybe you love hip-hop or classical music, or both. Of course, if you want to write more than twenty things, feel free.
   - Jot down ten to twenty things that you appreciate about yourself and why. If it's helpful, you can also draw on favorable remarks that others have made about you as a place to get ideas, and then think about whether you agree.
   - Think about a time when you aspired to reach a goal that was personally meaningful for you, and you did it. Write that moment down in detail, including what you did and how you felt. How does it make you feel now?

EPILOGUE

Thank you for joining me on this tour through diverse gardens of denial and the pathways we create through them by turning down the dial. At this juncture, it seems fitting to reflect on why we took this tour, what we got out of it, and where we go from here as a way of taking a broader perspective on our journey. Hopefully, this will help us layer a kind of meaning and significance on our travels that is uniquely our own.

To begin, consider why you originally chose to take this tour. After all, you didn't have to buy this book, open it, start reading, or continue until the end, right? Don't get me wrong; I'm deeply grateful that you did all of these things! What I mean is, to be willing to make the commitment to finish the tour, there was something you hoped to get out of it. Perhaps you had heard that denial was wrong or unhealthy, and so you wanted to explore it more and reach your own conclusion. Maybe you've had a mixed relationship with denial, and you weren't sure whether to hold on to it or to find a way to break through it. Or perhaps you have loved ones who are wrestling with denial, and you were hoping to understand them better or help them in some way. Regardless of what they may be, your reasons for taking this tour and staying on it will help you gauge whether you got what you came for. My earnest wish is that you did and are able to move forward with the sense that your journey was relevant, helpful, and ultimately a worthwhile investment of time and energy.

As you look back, you might ask what overarching takeaway message you got out of this experience, the one that ties everything together. Thanks to each of us being delightfully unique and having different perspectives and needs, we will see different angles on it all and find different parts of the journey more valuable than others. For my part, the essential idea that motivated me to write this book is the importance of balance in how we use denial.

Unfortunately, denial has a bad reputation that it doesn't deserve. I noted early on how, when people say that someone is *in denial,* they almost always mean this disapprovingly. As we witnessed repeatedly on this tour, there are certainly times when turning down the dial is detrimental, holding the potential to sabotage us and whittle away at the joy in life. We saw how we can go too far with it, using denial in ways that can, ironically, bring us more of the very thing we're trying to evade.

But I also hope you got the message that saying denial is *capable* of pulling us underwater is not the same as saying that denial is *inherently* harmful. It is my belief that it's time for that notion to go away because, as we've seen repeatedly, there are also times that we need to be able to be *in* denial, times when denial truly can be a loyal friend, ever prepared to lend us a hand when we need it to get through life's struggles. Fundamentally, I see denial as a tool, and the key with any tool is to use it in beneficial ways that serve us. Reality offers us many gifts, comforts, and joys, but it bites, burns, and even tortures us too. A measure of denial gives us a bit of added insulation against reality's heat. To the best of my knowledge, there's no rule in life stating that we always need to face every painful experience with full force, minus any protective layering, in order to be a strong, whole, human being.

Just consider other tools we use for our welfare and security. Would you grab hot pans fresh out of the stove with your bare hands, insisting that it's healthy and courageous to embrace the scalding sensation rather than hide behind oven mitts? In the winter, would you say that your ability to walk around in a freezing blizzard wearing only a T-shirt and shorts, with no shoes or coat, is a measure of your personal strength and toughness because you can fully face the icy cold? If you did, you'd be rewarded with chapped hands, frostbite, and hypothermia. The same is true with denial. A healthy layer of padding affords us the ability to dose ourselves when reality is too harsh, allowing us to determine just how much we take on and helping us adapt and thrive as a result, even in the face of dire circumstances. We just don't want to don those mitts at all times, or wear our winter coat in all seasons, because then, in our attempt to shield ourselves from any discomfort, we'd lose the capacity to expose ourselves to life as fully as we can. We need some discomfort to stretch ourselves and grow, and we flourish with experiences that lift us up out of the depths and bring gratification and happiness. Fortunately, denial in good measure lends us a hand toward both.

And so it is that we have explored on this tour how we can break patterns of denial that aren't serving us, and how we can turn down the dial in ways that will enrich our life. I hope that you will continue to listen to yourself, paying attention to where your dial is set at different levels of your life and noticing whether each setting helps or hinders you. You will, like all of us, stumble and find yourself turning your own dial in ways that don't help you, whether that's too much or not enough. I encourage you to be patient with yourself, to not expect perfection, and to allow room for a hearty splash of humor and curious exploration as you continue developing your ability to sensibly tune your own personal dial in ways that lift you up. And as we say goodbye, I sincerely wish that you will enjoy a lifelong journey of making your life brighter, embracing it with all that you have.

That's what truly matters in the end.

RESOURCES

As you move forward from our tour of turning down the dial, you may find yourself wanting to learn more about specific topics we covered, to take the next step in making changes in your life, or to reach out for help. I hope the resources listed here will help you do that. Whether or not you find what you're looking for here, I invite you to continue your search for other avenues of support and information. Examples include your partner, family members, friends, your primary care provider, clergy, mentors at school or work, local psychotherapists, discussion boards, and search engines. Wherever your journey in life takes you after reading this book, don't go it alone.

1. If you're thinking about giving therapy a try and would like to find a therapist:
   - American Psychological Association. Psychology Help Center. www.apa.org/helpcenter/index.aspx

2. For help with acknowledging, understanding, and working with emotions, and overcoming chronic emotional avoidance:
   - McLaren, K. (2010). *The Language of Emotions: What Your Feelings Are Trying to Tell You.* Boulder, CO: Sounds True.
   - Goleman, D. (2005). *Emotional Intelligence: Why It Can Matter More than IQ.* New York: Bantam Dell.
   - Greenspan, M. (2004). *Healing Through the Dark Emotions: The Wisdom of Grief, Fear, and Despair.* Boston: Shambhala Publications.
   - McKay, M., Fanning, P., & Ona, P. E. Z. (2011). *Mind and Emotions: A Universal Treatment for Emotional Disorders.* Oakland, CA: New Harbinger Publications.

3. For help coping with illness and physical pain:
   - Donoghue, P. J., & Siegel, M. E. (2012). *Sick and Tired of Feeling Sick and Tired: Living with Invisible Chronic Illness.* New York: W.W. Norton & Company.
   - Lynn, J., Harrold, J., Schuster, J. L. (2011). *Handbook for Mortals: Guidance for People Facing Serious Illness.* New York: Oxford University Press.
   - Bernhard, T. (2015). *How to Live Well with Chronic Pain and Illness: A Mindful Guide.* Somerville, MA: Wisdom Publications.

4. For help coping with trauma and PTSD, or to help someone facing trauma and PTSD:
   - Raja, S. (2012). *Overcoming Trauma and PTSD: A Workbook Integrating Skills from ACT, DBT, and CBT.* Oakland, CA: New Harbinger Publications.
   - Rothschild, B. (2010). *8 Keys to Safe Trauma Recovery: Take-Charge Strategies to Empower Your Healing.* New York: W.W. Norton & Company.
   - Birch, B. B. (2014). *Yoga for Warriors: Basic Training in Strength, Resilience, and Peace of Mind.* Boulder, CO: Sounds True.
   - Matsakis, A. T. (2014). *Loving Someone with PTSD: A Practical Guide to Understanding and Connecting with Your Partner after Trauma.* Oakland, CA: New Harbinger Publications.

5. For information on growth after trauma:
   - Joseph, S. (2013). *What Doesn't Kill Us: The New Psychology of Posttraumatic Growth.* New York: Basic Books.
   - Rendon, J. (2015). *Upside: The New Science of Post-Traumatic Growth.* New York: Touchstone.

6. For help with alcohol misuse:
   - Farren, C. (2011). *Overcoming Alcohol Misuse: A 28-Day Guide.* Dublin: Orpen Press.
   - Rotgers, F., Kern, M. F., & Hoeltzel, R. (2002). *Responsible Drinking: A Moderation Management Approach for Problem Drinkers.* Oakland, CA: New Harbinger Publications.

7. For help with addiction, or to help someone who struggles with addiction:
   - Glasner-Edwards, S. (2015). *The Addiction Recovery Skills Workbook: Changing Addictive Behaviors Using CBT, Mindfulness, and Motivational Interviewing Techniques.* Oakland, CA: New Harbinger Publications.
   - Dodes, L. M. (2002). *The Heart of Addiction: A New Approach to Understanding and Managing Alcoholism and Other Addictive Behaviors.* New York: William Morrow Paperbacks.
   - Peltz, L. (2013). *The Mindful Path to Addiction Recovery: A Practical Guide to Regaining Control over Your Life.* Boston: Shambhala Publications.

- Foote, J., Wilkens, C., Kosanke, N., & Higgs, S. (2014). *Beyond Addiction: How Science and Kindness Help People Change.* New York: Scribner.
- Berg, B. (2014). *Loving Someone in Recovery: The Answers You Need When Your Partner Is Recovering from Addiction.* Oakland, CA: New Harbinger Publications.

8. For help with depression and anxiety:
   - Burns, D. D. (2008). *Feeling Good: The New Mood Therapy.* New York: HarperCollins.
   - Williams, M., Teasdale, J., Segal, Z., & Kabat-Zinn, J. (2007). *The Mindful Way through Depression: Freeing Yourself from Chronic Unhappiness.* New York: The Guilford Press.
   - Marra, T. (2004). *Depressed and Anxious: The Dialectical Behavior Therapy Workbook for Overcoming Depression & Anxiety.* Oakland, CA: New Harbinger Publications.

9. For more information on unconscious attitudes and feelings:
   - Mlodinow, L. (2013). *Subliminal: How Your Unconscious Mind Rules Your Behavior.* New York: First Vintage Books.
   - Gigerenzer, G. (2008). *Gut Feelings: The Intelligence of the Unconscious.* New York: Penguin Books.
   - Wilson, T. D. (2004). *Strangers to Ourselves: Discovering the Adaptive Unconscious.* Cambridge, MA: Harvard University Press.

10. To increase your acceptance of yourself and enhance your self-esteem:
    - Brown, B. (2010). *The Gifts of Imperfection: Let Go of Who You Think You're Supposed to Be and Embrace Who You Are.* Center City, MN: Hazelden.
    - Ashear, V. (2015). *Self-Acceptance: The Key to Recovery from Mental Illness.* Las Vegas: Central Recovery Press.
    - Marotta, J. (2013). *50 Mindful Steps to Self-Esteem: Everyday Practices for Cultivating Self-Acceptance and Self-Compassion.* Oakland, CA: New Harbinger Publications.
    - Schiraldi, G. R. (2001). *The Self-Esteem Workbook.* Oakland, CA: New Harbinger Publications.

11. To learn more about mindfulness meditation and find classes near you:

- Gunaratana, B. H. (2011). *Mindfulness in Plain English.* Somerville, MA: Wisdom Publications.
- Kabat-Zinn, J. (2005). *Wherever You Go, There You Are.* Boston: Hachette Books.
- MeditationFinder.Com. www.meditationfinder.com

12. To learn more about willpower and delaying gratification:

- Mischel, W. (2015). *The Marshmallow Test: Why Self-Control Is the Engine of Success.* New York: Little, Brown and Company.
- McGonigal, K. (2013). *The Willpower Instinct: How Self-Control Works, Why It Matters, and What You Can Do to Get More of It.* New York: Penguin Books.

13. To develop more gratitude:

- Lesowitz, N., & Sammons, M. B. (2009). *Living Life as a Thank You: The Transformative Power of Daily Gratitude.* Jersey City, NJ: Viva Editions.
- Emmons, R. (2008). *Thanks!: How Practicing Gratitude Can Make You Happier.* New York: Houghton Mifflin.
- Arrien, A. (2013). *Living in Gratitude: Mastering the Art of Giving Thanks Every Day, A Month-by-Month Guide.* Boulder, CO: Sounds True.

14. To learn more about attachment and romantic relationships:

- Levine, A., & Heller, R. (2012). *Attached: The New Science of Adult Attachment and How It Can Help You Find—and Keep—Love.* New York: TarcherPerigee.
- Johnson, S. (2008). *Hold Me Tight: Seven Conversations for a Lifetime of Love.* New York: Little, Brown, and Company.

15. To enhance your romantic relationships:

- McKay, M., Fanning, P., & Paleg, K. (2006). *Couple Skills: Making Your Relationship Work.* Oakland, CA: New Harbinger Publications.
- Gottman, J. M., & Silver, N. (2015). *The Seven Principles for Making Marriage Work: A Practical Guide from the Country's Foremost Relationship Expert.* New York: Harmony Books.

16. For help if you're ambivalent about your relationship:
    - Kirshenbaum, M. (1997). *Too Good to Leave, Too Bad to Stay: A Step-by-Step Guide to Help You Decide Whether to Stay In or Get Out of Your Relationship.* New York: Plume.

17. For help if you're in an abusive relationship, if you're wondering if you're being abused, or if you're engaging in abuse and want to stop:
    - Evans, P. (2010). *The Verbally Abusive Relationship: How to Recognize It and How to Respond.* Avon, MA: Adams Media.
    - Engel, B. (2003). *The Emotionally Abusive Relationship: How to Stop Being Abused and How to Stop Abusing.* Hoboken, NJ: John Wiley & Sons.
    - Hunter, J. V. (2010). *But He'll Change: End the Thinking That Keeps You in an Abusive Relationship.* Center City, MN: Hazelden.
    - Donaldson, C., & Flood, R. (2006). *Stop Hurting the Woman You Love: Breaking the Cycle of Abusive Behavior.* Center City, MN: Hazelden.

18. For help if you feel physically unsafe in your relationship and are afraid of your partner:
    - American Psychological Association. Intimate Partner Violence: Facts and Resources. www.apa.org/topics/violence/partner.aspx
    - The National Domestic Violence Hotline (1-800-799-SAFE). Saving Lives, Giving Hope. www.thehotline.org

19. For help with workplace bullying:
    - Namie, G., & Namie, R. (2009). *The Bully at Work: What You Can Do to Stop the Hurt and Reclaim Your Dignity on the Job.* Naperville, IL: Sourcebooks.
    - Sutton, R. I. (2010). *The No Asshole Rule: Building a Civilized Workplace and Surviving One That Isn't.* New York: Grand Central Publishing.

20. For help with feeling more empowered over your choices and taking responsibility for the direction of your life:
    - Branden, N. (1997). *Taking Responsibility: Self-Reliance and the Accountable Life.* New York: Fireside.
    - Izzo, J. B. (2012). *Stepping Up: How Taking Responsibility Changes Everything.* San Francisco: Berrett-Koehler Publishers.

- Beattie, M. (2010). *Choices: Taking Control of Your Life and Making It Matter.* San Francisco: HarperOne.
- Schwartz, B. (2005). *The Paradox of Choice: Why More Is Less.* New York: Harper Perennial.

21. For more information on navigating risk in life:
    - Gigerenzer, G. (2015). *Risk Savvy: How to Make Good Decisions.* New York: Penguin Books.
    - Gigerenzer, G. (2003). *Reckoning with Risk: Learning to Live with Uncertainty.* London: Penguin Books.
    - Gill, L. (2009). *You Unstuck: Mastering the New Rules of Risk-Taking in Work and Life.* Palo Alto, CA: Travelers' Tales/Solas House.
    - Heath, R. (2009). *Celebrating Failure: The Power of Taking Risks, Making Mistakes, and Thinking Big.* Pompton Plains, NJ: Career Press.

22. For information on beliefs we hold that can downplay our sense of vulnerability to harm, and that trauma or extreme hardship can contradict:
    - Janoff-Bulman, R. (2002). *Shattered Assumptions: Towards a New Psychology of Trauma.* New York: Free Press.

23. For information on optimism and positive thinking:
    - Seligman, M. E. P. (2006). *Learned Optimism: How to Change Your Mind to Change Your Life.* New York: Vintage Books.
    - Peale, N. V. (2003). *The Power of Positive Thinking.* New York: Touchstone.
    - Fredrickson, B. (2009). *Positivity: Top-Notch Research Reveals the Upward Spiral That Will Change Your Life.* New York: Three Rivers Press.

24. For help with procrastination:
    - Tracy, B. (2007). *Eat That Frog!: 21 Great Ways to Stop Procrastinating and Get More Done in Less Time.* San Francisco: Berrett-Koehler Publishers.
    - Burka, J. B., & Yuen, L. M. (2008). *Procrastination: Why You Do It, What to Do About It Now.* Boston: Da Capo Press.
    - Pychyl, T. A. (2013). *Solving the Procrastination Puzzle: A Concise Guide to Strategies for Change.* New York: TarcherPerigee.

25. To cultivate compassion for others and yourself:
    - Ricard, M. (2015). *Altruism: The Power of Compassion to Change Yourself and the World.* New York: Little, Brown and Company.
    - Gilbert, P., & Choden. (2014). *Mindful Compassion: How the Science of Compassion Can Help You Understand Your Emotions, Live in the Present, and Connect Deeply with Others.* Oakland, CA: New Harbinger Publications.
    - Bekoff, M. (2010). *The Animal Manifesto: Six Reasons for Expanding Our Compassion Footprint.* Novato, CA: New World Library.

26. To learn about the four immeasurables:
    - Wallace, B. A. (2010). *The Four Immeasurables: Practices to Open the Heart.* Boston: Shambhala Publications.

27. To learn more about climate change and climate change denial:
    - Nye, B. (2015). *Unstoppable: Harnessing Science to Change the World.* New York: St. Martin's Press.
    - Marshall, G. (2015). *Don't Even Think About It: Why Our Brains Are Wired to Ignore Climate Change.* New York: Bloomsbury.
    - Oreskes, N., & Conway, E. M. (2011). *Merchants of Doubt: How a Handful of Scientists Obscured the Truth on Issues from Tobacco Smoke to Global Warming.* New York: Bloomsbury USA.

28. To learn more about unconscious biases, stereotypes, and isms:
    - Ross, H. J. (2014). *Everyday Bias: Identifying and Navigating Unconscious Judgments in Our Daily Lives.* Lanham, MD: Rowman & Littlefield Publishers.
    - Banaji, M. R., & Greenwald, A. G. (2013). *Blindspot: Hidden Biases of Good People.* New York: Delacorte Press.
    - Steele, C. M. (2011). *Whistling Vivaldi: How Stereotypes Affect Us and What We Can Do.* New York: W.W. Norton & Company.
    - Bonilla-Silva, E. (2013). *Racism without Racists: Color-Blind Racism and the Persistence of Racial Inequality in America.* Lanham, MD: Rowman & Littlefield Publishers.
    - To discover your own implicit attitudes, you can take the Implicit Association Test through Project Implicit. https://implicit.harvard.edu/implicit

29. To make changes in your lifestyle:

- Arloski, M. (2014). *Wellness Coaching for Lasting Lifestyle Change.* Duluth, MN: Whole Person Associates.
- Duhigg, C. (2014). *The Power of Habit: Why We Do What We Do in Life and Business.* New York: Random House.

30. To explore fear of aging, assumptions about aging, and aging successfully:

- Karpf, A. (2015). *How to Age.* New York: Picador.
- Valliant, G. E. (2003). *Aging Well. New York*: Little, Brown and Company.
- Schachter-Shalomi, Z., & Miller, R. S. (2014). *From Age-ing to Sage-ing: A Revolutionary Approach to Growing Older.* New York: Grand Central Publishing.

31. To explore fear and denial of dying:

- Becker, E. (1997). *The Denial of Death.* New York: Free Press.
- Hanh, T. N. (2003). *No Death, No Fear: Comforting Wisdom for Life.* New York: Riverhead Books.

NOTES

Chapter One: If Denial Ain't Just a River, Then What Is It?

1. Kortte, K. B., & Wegener, S. T. (2004). Denial of illness in medical rehabilitation populations: Theory, research, and definition. *Rehabilitation Psychology, 49,* 187–199.
2. Moyer, A., & Levine, E. G. (1998). Clarification of the conceptualization and measurement of denial in psychosocial oncology research. *Annals of Behavioral Medicine, 20,* 149–160.
3. For information on the complex and multidimensional nature of denial: Goldbeck, R. (1997). Denial in physical illness. *Journal of Psychosomatic Research, 43,* 575–593; Kortte, K. B., & Wegener, S. T. (2004). Denial of illness in medical rehabilitation populations: Theory, research, and definition. *Rehabilitation Psychology, 49,* 187–199; Livneh, H. (2009). Denial of chronic illness and disability: Part II. Research findings, measurement considerations, and clinical aspects. *Rehabilitation Counseling Bulletin, 53,* 44–55; and Thompson, S. C., & Schlehofer, M. M. (2008). Control, denial, and heightened sensitivity reactions to personal threat: Testing the generalizability of the threat orientation approach. *Personality and Social Psychology Bulletin, 34,* 1070–1083.
4. For information on types of denial: Goldbeck, R. (1997). Denial in physical illness. *Journal of Psychosomatic Research, 43,* 575–593; Johnson, S. D., & Williams, L. B. (2005). Deference, denial, and exclusion: Men talk about contraception and unintended pregnancy. *International Journal of Men's Health, 4,* 223–242; Levine, J., Rudy, T., & Kerns, R. (1994). A two factor model of denial of illness: A confirmatory factor analysis. *Journal of Psychosomatic Research, 38,* 99–110; and Warrenburg, S., Levine, J., Schwartz, G. E., Fontana, A. F., Kerns, R. D., Delaney, R., & Mattson, R. (1989). Defensive coping and blood pressure reactivity in medical patients. *Journal of Behavioral Medicine, 12,* 407–424.
5. For information on avoidance: Sweeny, K., Melnyk, D., Miller, W., & Shepperd, J. A. (2010). Information avoidance: Who, what, when, and why. *Review of General Psychology, 14,* 340–353.
6. Ibid.
7. These remaining examples of information avoidance come from Sweeny, K., Melnyk, D., Miller, W., & Shepperd, J. A. (2010). Information avoidance: Who, what, when, and why. *Review of General Psychology, 14,* 340–353.
8. Ibid.

9. For all three positive illusions we're covering here: Taylor, S. E., & Brown, J. D. (1988). Illusion and well-being: A social psychological perspective on mental health. *Psychological Bulletin, 103,* 193–210.
10. Vincze, A. E., Roth, M., & Degi, L. C. (2012). Self-enhancement relationship to cognitive schemas and psychological distress in young adults. *Journal of Cognitive and Behavioral Psychotherapies, 12,* 189–207.
11. Goldbeck, R. (1997). Denial in physical illness. *Journal of Psychosomatic Research, 43,* 575–593.
12. For these three reasons: Sweeny, K., Melnyk, D., Miller, W., & Shepperd, J. A. (2010). Information avoidance: Who, what, when, and why. *Review of General Psychology, 14,* 340–353.
13. Ibid.
14. Ibid.
15. Ibid.

Chapter Two: Denial within Us

1. Woo, C-W., Roy, M., Buhle, J. T., & Wagner, T. D. (2015). Distinct brain systems mediate the effects of nociceptive input and self-regulation on pain. *PLoS Biology, 13*(1). doi:10.1371/journal.pbio.1002036
2. Wiederhold, B. K., Soomro, A., Riva, G., & Wiederhold, M. D. (2014). Future directions: Advances and implications of virtual environments designed for pain management. *Cyberpsychology, Behavior, and Social Networking, 17,* 414–422.
3. Duschek, S., Werner, N. S., del Paso, G. A. R, & Schandry, R. (2015). The contributions of interoceptive awareness to cognitive and affective facets of body experience. *Journal of Individual Differences, 36,* 110–118.
4. Centers for Disease Control and Prevention. (2015, October 6). Common colds: Protect yourself and others. Retrieved from www.cdc.gov/features/rhinoviruses
5. Sources for information on how denial can be a healthy form of coping: Ellis, J., Lloyd Williams, M., Wagland, R., Bailey, C., & Molassiotis, A. (2013). Coping with and factors impacting upon the experience of lung cancer in patients and primary carers. *European Journal of Cancer Care, 22,* 97–106; and Vos, M. S., & de Haes, J. C. J. M. (2007). Denial in cancer patients, an explorative review. *Psycho-Oncology, 16*(1), 12–25.
6. Ellis, J., Lloyd Williams, M., Wagland, R., Bailey, C., & Molassiotis, A. (2013). Coping with and factors impacting upon the experience of lung cancer in patients and primary carers. *European Journal of Cancer Care, 22,* 97–106.
7. Barlow, M. A., Liu, S. Y., & Wrosch, C. (2015). Chronic illness and loneliness in older adulthood: The role of self-protective control strategies. *Health Psychology, 34,* 870–879.
8. Ibid.

9. Johnston, L. B. (2014). Surviving critical illness: New insights from mixed-methods research. *Smith College Studies in Social Work, 84,* 76–106.
10. Musich, S., Ozminkowski, R. J., Bottone, F. G., Jr., Hawkins, K., Wang, S. S., Ekness, J. G., . . . Yeh, C. S. (2014). Barriers to managing coronary artery disease among older women. *Journal of Women and Aging, 26*(2), 146–159.
11. Lyimo, R. A., Stutterheim, S. E., Hospers, H. J., de Glee, T., van der Ven, A., & de Bruin, M. (2014). Stigma, disclosure, coping, and medication adherence among people living with HIV/AIDS in Northern Tanzania. *AIDS Patient Care and STDs, 28,* 98–105.
12. Many thanks to Dr. Joshua Rackley, who photographed the shark and generously gave the image to me.
13. Kim, M. Y., Ford, B. Q., Mauss, I., & Tamir, M. (2015). Knowing when to seek anger: Psychological health and context-sensitive emotional preferences. *Cognition and Emotion, 29,* 1126–1136.
14. Ibid.
15. Machell, K. A., Goodman, F. R., & Kashdan, T. B. (2015). Experiential avoidance and well-being: A daily diary analysis. *Cognition and Emotion, 29,* 351–359.
16. Hinds, E., Jones, L. B., Gau, J. M., Forrester, K. K., & Biglan, A. (2015). Teacher distress and the role of experiential avoidance. *Psychology in the Schools, 52,* 284–297.
17. Gilbert, P., McEwan, K., Catarino, F., Baiao, R., & Palmeira, L. (2014). Fears of happiness and compassion in relationship with depression, alexithymia, and attachment security in a depressed sample. *British Journal of Clinical Psychology, 53,* 228–244.
18. Ibid.
19. For information on link between emotions and healing after trauma: O'Bryan, E. M., McLeish, A. C., Kraemer, K. M., & Fleming, J. B. (2015). Emotion regulation difficulties and posttraumatic stress disorder symptom cluster severity among trauma-exposed college students. *Psychological Trauma: Theory, Research, Practice, and Policy, 7,* 131–137; and Reddy, M. K., Seligowski, A. V., Rabenhorst, M. M., & Orcutt, H. K. (2015). Predictors of expressive writing content and posttraumatic stress following a mass shooting. *Psychological Trauma: Theory, Research, Practice, and Policy, 7,* 286–294.
20. Meier, S. T. (2014). Rediscovering the role of avoidance in psychotherapy progress and outcome. *Professional Psychology: Research and Practice, 45,* 212–217.
21. Riley, B. (2014). Experiential avoidance mediates the association between thought suppression and mindfulness with problem gambling. *Journal of Gambling Studies, 30,* 163–171.

22. Hagstrom, D., & Kaldo, V. (2014). Escapism among players of MMORPGs—Conceptual clarification, its relation to mental health factors, and development of a new measure. *Cyberpsychology, Behavior, and Social Networking, 17,* 19–25.
23. Stotts, A. L., Vujanovic, A., Heads, A., Suchting, R., Green, C. E., & Schmitz, J. M. (2015). The role of avoidance and inflexibility in characterizing response to contingency management for cocaine use disorders: A secondary profile analysis. *Psychology of Addictive Behaviors, 29,* 408–413.
24. Stoddard Dare, P. A., & Derigne, L. (2010). Denial in alcohol and other drug use disorders: A critique of theory. *Addiction Research and Theory, 18,* 181–193.
25. Witvliet, C. V., Hofelich Mohr, A. J., Hinman, N. G., & Knoll, R. W. (2015). Transforming or restraining rumination: The impact of compassionate reappraisal versus emotion suppression on empathy, forgiveness, and affective psychophysiology. *The Journal of Positive Psychology, 10,* 248–261.
26. Brooks, A. W. (2014). Get excited: Reappraising pre-performance anxiety as excitement. *Journal of Experimental Psychology: General, 143,* 1144–1158.
27. Gilbert, R. (n.d.). Quote. Retrieved from www.goodreads.com/quotes/117212-it-s-all-right-to-have-butterflies-in-your-stomach-just
28. Christou-Champi, S., Farrow, T. F. D., & Webb, T. L. (2015). Automatic control of negative emotions: Evidence that structured practice increases the efficiency of emotion regulation. *Cognition and Emotion, 29*(2), 319–331.
29. Carlson, K. A., Wolfe, J., Blanchard, S. J., Huber, J. C., & Ariely, D. (2015). The budget contraction effect: How contracting budgets lead to less varied choice. *Journal of Marketing Research, 52,* 337–348.
30. Ibid.
31. Ratliff, K. A., & Howell, J. L. (2015). Implicit prototypes predict risky sun behavior. *Health Psychology, 34,* 231–242.
32. Ibid.
33. Walsh, E. M., & Kiviniemi, M. T. (2014). Changing how I feel about the food: Experimentally manipulated affective associations with fruits change fruit choice behaviors. *Journal of Behavioral Medicine, 37,* 322–331.
34. Kidwell, B., Hasford, J., & Hardesty, D. M. (2015). Emotional ability training and mindful eating. *Journal of Marketing Research, 52,* 105–119.
35. Ibid.
36. Ibid.
37. Dickter, C. L., Forestell, C. A., Hammett, P. J., & Young, C. M. (2014). Relationship between alcohol dependence, escape drinking, and early

neural attention to alcohol-related cues. *Psychopharmacology, 231,* 2031–2040.

38. Yang, L., Zhang, J., & Zhao, X. (2015). Implicit processing of heroin and emotional cues in abstinent heroin users: Early and late event-related potential effects. *The American Journal of Drug and Alcohol Abuse, 41,* 237–245.
39. For information on how things related to alcohol and other drugs can pull attention and increase the odds of craving and potential for relapse: Drummond, C. D. (2000). What does cue-reactivity have to offer clinical research? *Addiction, 95,* 129–144; Field, M., & Cox, W. M. (2008). Attentional bias in addictive behaviors: A review of its development, causes, and consequences. *Drug and Alcohol Dependence, 97,* 1–20; and Yang, L., Zhang, J., & Zhao, X. (2015). Implicit processing of heroin and emotional cues in abstinent heroin users: Early and late event-related potential effects. *The American Journal of Drug and Alcohol Abuse, 41,* 237–245.
40. Wolff, N., von Hippel, C., Brener, L., & von Hippel, W. (2015). Implicit identification with drug and alcohol use predicts retention in residential rehabilitation programs. *Psychology of Addictive Behaviors, 29,* 136–141.
41. Damen, T. G. E., van Baaren, R. B., Brass, M., Aarts, H., & Dijksterhuis, A. (2015). Put your plan into action: The influence of action plans on agency and responsibility. *Journal of Personality and Social Psychology, 108,* 850–866.
42. Park, J. K., & John, D. R. (2014). I think I can, I think I can: Brand use, self-efficacy, and performance. *Journal of Marketing Research, 51,* 233–247.
43. Job, V., Bernecker, K., Miketta, S., & Friese, M. (2015). Implicit theories about willpower predict the activation of a rest goal following self-control exertion. *Journal of Personality and Social Psychology, 109,* 694–706.
44. Coulter, K. S., & Grewal, D. (2014). Name-letters and birthday-numbers: Implicit egotism effects in pricing. *Journal of Marketing, 78,* 102–120.
45. Lawson, R. (2015). I just love the attention: Implicit preference for direct eye contact. *Visual Cognition, 23,* 450–488.

Chapter Three: Denial at the Level of Ourselves

1. For information on the damaging impact of avoiding upsetting memories, as well as other thoughts and feelings: Hayes, S. C., & Gifford, E. V. (1997). The trouble with language: Experiential avoidance, rules, and the nature of verbal events. *Psychological Science, 8,* 170–173.
2. Dulin, P. L., & Passmore, T. (2010). Avoidance of potentially traumatic stimuli mediates the relationship between accumulated lifetime trauma

and late-life depression and anxiety. *Journal of Traumatic Stress, 23,* 296–299.

3. Hayes, S. C., & Gifford, E. V. (1997). The trouble with language: Experiential avoidance, rules, and the nature of verbal events. *Psychological Science, 8,* 170–173.
4. Eisma, M. C., Stroebe, M. S., Schut, H. A. W., Stroebe, W., Boelen, P. A., & van den Bout, J. (2013). Avoidance processes mediate the relationship between rumination and symptoms of complicated grief and depression following loss. *Journal of Abnormal Psychology, 122,* 961–970.
5. For information on the relationship between painful memories, PTSD, depression, and substance use: Chopko, B. A., Palmieri, P. A., & Adams, R. E. (2013). Associations between police stress and alcohol use: Implications for practice. *Journal of Loss and Trauma, 18,* 482–497; and O'Kearney, R., & Parry, L. (2014). Comparative physiological reactivity during script-driven recall in depression and posttraumatic stress disorder. *Journal of Abnormal Psychology, 123,* 523–532.
6. Lee, A., & Ji, L. (2014). Moving away from a bad past and toward a good future: Feelings influence the metaphorical understanding of time. *Journal of Experimental Psychology: General, 143*(1), 21–26.
7. Kross, E., & Ayduk, O. (2011). Making meaning out of negative experiences by self-distancing. *Current Directions in Psychological Science, 20,* 187–191.
8. Alparone, F. R., Pagliaro, S., & Rizzo, I. (2015). The words to tell their own pain: Linguistic markers of cognitive reappraisal in mediating benefits of expressive writing. *Journal of Social and Clinical Psychology, 34,* 495–507.
9. He, J., van de Vijver, F. J. R., Espinosa, A. D., Abubakar, A., Dimitrova, R., Adams, B. G., . . . Villieux, A. (2015). Socially desirable responding: Enhancement and denial in 20 countries. *Cross-Cultural Research: The Journal of Comparative Social Science, 49,* 227–249.
10. Pan, C., Pettit, N. C., Sivanathan, N., & Blader, S. L. (2014). Low-status aversion: The effect of self-threat on willingness to buy and sell. *Journal of Applied Social Psychology, 44,* 708–716.
11. Quinn, D. M., & Chaudoir, S. R. (2015). Living with a concealable stigmatized identity: The impact of anticipated stigma, centrality, salience, and cultural stigma on psychological distress and health. *Stigma and Health, 1,* 35–59.
12. Critcher, C. R., & Ferguson, M. J. (2014). The cost of keeping it hidden: Decomposing concealment reveals what makes it depleting. *Journal of Experimental Psychology: General, 143,* 721–735.
13. Keene, D. E., Cowan, S. K., & Baker, A. C. (2015). "When you're in a crisis like that, you don't want people to know": Mortgage strain, stigma, and mental health. *American Journal of Public Health, 105,* 1008–1012.

14. Martin, A., & Fisher, C. D. (2014). Understanding and improving managers' responses to employee depression. *Industrial and Organizational Psychology: Perspectives on Science and Practice, 7,* 270–274.
15. Maier, J. A., Gentile, D. A., Vogel, D. L., & Kaplan, S. A. (2014). Media influences on self-stigma of seeking psychological services: The importance of media portrayals and person perception. *Psychology of Popular Media Culture, 3,* 239–256.
16. Lannin, D. G., Vogel, D. L., Brenner, R. E., & Tucker, J. R. (2015). Predicting self-esteem and intentions to seek counseling: The internalized stigma model. *The Counseling Psychologist, 43,* 64–93.
17. Wade, N. G., Vogel, D. L., Armistead-Jehle, P., Meit, S. S., Heath, P. J., & Strass, H. A. (2015). Modeling stigma, help-seeking attitudes, and intentions to seek behavioral healthcare in a clinical military sample. *Psychiatric Rehabilitation Journal, 38,* 135–141.
18. Martinez, A. G. (2014). When "they" become "I": Ascribing humanity to mental illness influences treatment-seeking for mental/behavioral health conditions. *Journal of Social and Clinical Psychology, 33,* 187–206.
19. Cerezo, A., Morales, A., Quintero, D., & Rothman, S. (2014). Trans migrations: Exploring life at the intersection of transgender identity and immigration. *Psychology of Sexual Orientation and Gender Diversity, 1,* 170–180.
20. Yousef, O., Popat, A., & Hunter, M. S. (2015). An investigation of masculinity attitudes, gender, and attitudes toward psychological help-seeking. *Psychology of Men & Masculinity, 16,* 234–237.
21. Sloan, C., Conner, M., & Gough, B. (2015). How does masculinity impact on health? A quantitative study of masculinity and health behavior in a sample of UK men and women. *Psychology of Men & Masculinity, 16,* 206–217.
22. Cheryan, S., Cameron, J. S., Katagiri, Z., & Monin, B. (2015). Manning up: Threatened men compensate by disavowing feminine references and embracing masculine attributes. *Social Psychology, 46,* 218–227.
23. Clarke, M. J., Marks, A. D. G., & Lykins, A. D. (2015). Effects of normative masculinity on males' dysfunctional sexual beliefs, sexual attitudes, and perceptions of sexual functioning. *Journal of Sex Research, 52,* 327–337.
24. Granato, S. L., Smith, P. N., & Selwyn, C. N. (2015). Acquired capability and masculine gender norm adherence: Potential pathways to higher rates of male suicide. *Psychology of Men & Masculinity, 16,* 246–153.
25. Wessel, J. L., Hagiwara, N., Ryan, A. M., & Kermond, C. M. Y. (2015). Should women applicants "man up" for traditionally masculine fields? Effectiveness of two verbal identity management strategies. *Psychology of Women Quarterly, 39,* 243–255.

26. Wakefield, J. R. H., Hopkins, N., & Greenwood, R. M. (2012). Thanks but no thanks: Women's avoidance of help-seeking in the context of a dependency-related stereotype. *Psychology of Women Quarterly, 36,* 423–431.
27. Roberts, L. M., Cha, S. E., & Kim, S. S. (2014). Strategies for managing impressions of racial identity in the workplace. *Cultural Diversity and Ethnic Minority Psychology, 20,* 529–540.
28. Kwate, N. O. A., & Goodman, M. S. (2015). Cross-sectional and longitudinal effects of racism on mental health among residents of Black neighborhoods in New York City. *American Journal of Public Health, 105,* 711–718.
29. Watson, N. N., & Hunter, C. D. (2015). Anxiety and depression among African American women: The costs of strength and negative attitudes toward psychological help-seeking. *Cultural Diversity and Ethnic Minority Psychology, 21,* 604–612.
30. Puckett, J. A., Levitt, H. M., Horne, S. G., & Hayes-Skelton, S. A. (2015). Internalized heterosexism and psychological distress: The mediating roles of self-criticism and community connectedness. *Psychology of Sexual Orientation and Gender Diversity, 2,* 426–435.
31. Greene, D. C., & Britton, P. J. (2015). Predicting relationship commitment in gay men: Contributions of vicarious shame and internalized homophobia to the investment model. *Psychology of Men & Masculinity, 16,* 78–87.
32. Sharkey, J. D., Ruderman, M. A., Mayworm, A. M., Green, J. G., Furlong, M. J., Rivera, N., & Purisch, L. (2015). Psychosocial functioning of bullied youth who adopt versus deny the bully-victim label. *School Psychology Quarterly, 30,* 91–104.
33. Lemay, E. P., Jr., & O'Leary, K. (2012). Alleviating interpersonal suspicions of low self-esteem individuals: Negativity as honesty credentials. *Journal of Social and Clinical Psychology, 31,* 251–288.
34. Chai, S., & Cho, Y. (2011). Cognitions associated with recovery from alcohol dependence. *Japanese Psychological Research, 53,* 327–332.
35. Lee, J. K., Boyle, R. G., D'Silva, J., St. Claire, A. W., Whittet, M. N., & Kinney, A. M. (2013). Smoker identity among occasional smokers: Findings from Minnesota. *American Journal of Health Behavior, 37,* 525–530.
36. Guenther, C. L., Taylor, S. G., & Alicke, M. D. (2015). Differential reliance on performance outliers in athletic self-assessment. *Journal of Applied Social Psychology, 45,* 374–382.
37. Brummelman, E., Thomaes, S., de Castro, B. O., Overbeek, G., & Bushman, B. J. (2014). "That's not just beautiful—that's incredibly beautiful!": The adverse impact of inflated praise on children with low self-esteem. *Psychological Science, 25,* 728–735.

38. Milyavskaya, M., Nadolny, D., & Koestner, R. (2014). Where do self-concordant goals come from? The role of domain-specific psychological need satisfaction. *Personality and Social Psychology Bulletin, 40,* 700–711.
39. For an excellent discussion of our unconscious needs and wants, as well as ways we can aim for authentic and healthy needs and wants in life: Sheldon, K. M. (2014). Becoming oneself: The central role of self-concordant goal selection. *Personality and Social Psychology Review, 18,* 349–365.
40. For a description of these blind spots: Wilson, T. D., & Gilbert, D. T. (2005). Affective forecasting: Knowing what to want. *Current Directions in Psychological Science, 14,* 131–134.
41. For information on the value of connecting with your principles: Lekes, N., Hope, N. H., Gouvela, L., Koestner, R., & Philippe, F. L. (2012). Influencing value priorities and increasing well-being: The effects of reflecting on intrinsic values. *The Journal of Positive Psychology, 7,* 249–261.
42. Milyavskaya, M., Inzlicht, M., Hope, N., & Koestner, R. (2015). Saying "no" to temptation: Want-to motivation improves self-regulation by reducing temptation rather than by increasing self-control. *Journal of Personality and Social Psychology, 109,* 677–693.
43. Ntoumanis, N., Healy, L. C., Sedikides, C., Duda, J., Stewart, B., Smith, A., & Bond, J. (2014). When the going gets tough: The "why" of goal striving matters. *Journal of Personality, 82*(3), 225–236.
44. Sheldon, K. M., & Houser-Marko, L. (2001). Self-concordance, goal attainment, and the pursuit of happiness: Can there be an upward spiral? *Journal of Personality and Social Psychology, 80,* 152–165.
45. Kuykendall, L., Tay, L., & Ng, V. (2015). Leisure engagement and subjective well-being: A meta-analysis. *Psychological Bulletin, 141,* 364–403.
46. For the benefits of being able to delay gratification: Waegeman, A., Declerck, C. H., Boone, C., Van Hecke, W., & Parizel, P. M. (2014). Individual differences in self-control in a time discounting task: An fMRI study. *Journal of Neuroscience, Psychology, and Economics, 7,* 65–79.
47. DeSteno, D., Li, Y., Dickens, L., & Lerner, J. S. (2014). Gratitude: A tool for reducing economic impatience. *Psychological Science, 25,* 1262–1267.
48. For this entire piece on planning to resist traps: Wieber, F., Sezer, L. A., & Gollwitzer, P. M. (2014). Asking "why" helps action control by goals but not plans. *Motivation and Emotion, 38,* 65–78.
49. For the benefits and limitations of seeing yourself as a doer: Houser-Marko, L., & Sheldon, K. M. (2006). Motivating behavioral persistence: The self-as-doer construct. *Psychology and Social Psychology Bulletin, 32,* 1037–1049.

Chapter Four: Denial at the Level of Our Relationships

1. For information on how expectations impact romantic relationships: Denes, A. (2015). Genetic and individual influences on predictors of disclosure: Exploring variation in the oxytocin receptor gene and attachment security. *Communication Monographs, 82,* 113–133; and Hazan, C., & Shaver, P. (1987). Romantic love conceptualized as an attachment process. *Journal of Personality and Social Psychology, 52,* 511–524.
2. Overall, N. C., Fletcher, G. J. O., Simpson, J. A., & Fillo, J. (2015). Attachment insecurity, biased perceptions of romantic partners' negative emotions, and hostile relationship behavior. *Journal of Personality and Social Psychology, 108,* 730–749.
3. Overall, N. C., Girme, Y. U., Lemay, E. P., Jr., & Hammond, M. D. (2014). Attachment anxiety and reactions to relationship threat: The benefits and costs of inducing guilt in romantic partners. *Journal of Personality and Social Psychology, 106,* 235–256.
4. Sadikaj, G., Moskowitz, D. S., & Zuroff, D. C. (2015). Felt security in daily interactions as a mediator of the effect of attachment on relationship satisfaction. *European Journal of Personality, 29,* 187–200.
5. Brassard, A., Dupuy, E., Bergeron, S., & Shaver, P. R. (2015). Attachment insecurities and women's sexual function and satisfaction: The mediating roles of sexual self-esteem, sexual anxiety, and sexual assertiveness. *Journal of Sex Research, 52,* 110–119.
6. Stanton, S. C. E., & Campbell, L. (2014). Psychological and physiological predictors of health in romantic relationships: An attachment perspective. *Journal of Personality, 82,* 528–538.
7. Slotter, E. B., & Luchies, L. B. (2014). Relationship quality promotes the desire for closeness among distressed avoidantly attached individuals. *Personal Relationships, 21,* 22–34.
8. For a description of how people who dismiss intimacy react when they receive average and high levels of support: Girme, Y. U., Overall, N. C., Simpson, J. A., & Fletcher, G. J. O. (2015). "All or nothing": Attachment avoidance and the curvilinear effects of partner support. *Journal of Personality and Social Psychology, 108,* 450–475.
9. Hudson, N. W., Fraley, R. C., Brumbaugh, C. C., & Vicary, A. M. (2014). Coregulation in romantic partners' attachment styles: A longitudinal investigation. *Personality and Social Psychology Bulletin, 40,* 845–857.
10. Stewart, J. G., & Harkness, K. L. (2015). The interpersonal toxicity of excessive reassurance-seeking: Evidence from a longitudinal study of romantic relationships. *Journal of Social and Clinical Psychology, 34,* 392–410.
11. Kuster, M., Bernecker, K., Backes, S., Brandstatter, V., Nussbeck, F. W., Bradbury., T. N., . . . Bodenmann, G. (2015). Avoidance orientation and

the escalation of negative communication in intimate relationships. *Journal of Personality and Social Psychology, 109,* 262–275.

12. Liu, E., & Roloff, M. E. (2015). Exhausting silence: Emotional costs of withholding complaints. *Negotiation and Conflict Management Research, 8,* 25–40.
13. Manne, S. L., Kissane, D., Zaider, T., Kashy, D., Lee, D., Heckman, C., & Virtue, S. M. (2015). Holding back, intimacy, and psychological and relationship outcomes among couples coping with prostate cancer. *Journal of Family Psychology, 29,* 708–719.
14. For ways people hide affection and when it can be appropriate to do so: Carton, S. T., & Horan, S. M. (2014). A diary examination of romantic and sexual partners withholding affectionate messages. *Journal of Social and Personal Relationships, 31,* 221–246.
15. For information on relationship happiness: Dainton, M. (2000). Maintenance behaviors, expectations for maintenance, and satisfaction: Linking comparison levels to relational maintenance strategies. *Journal of Social and Personal Relationships, 17,* 827–842; and Young, V., Curran, M., & Totenhagen, C. (2012). A daily diary study: Working to change the relationship and relational uncertainty in understanding positive relationship quality. *Journal of Social and Personal Relationships, 30,* 132–148.
16. Righetti, F., Kumashiro, M., & Campbell, S. B. (2014). Goal difficulty and openness to interpersonal goal support. *Personality and Social Psychology Bulletin, 40,* 1107–1118.
17. Lannin, D. G., Bittner, K. E., & Lorenz, F. O. (2013). Longitudinal effect of defensive denial on relationship instability. *Journal of Family Psychology, 27,* 968–977.
18. Langer, J. K., & Rodebaugh, T. L. (2013). Social anxiety and gaze avoidance: Averting gaze but not anxiety. *Cognitive Therapy Research, 37,* 1110–1120.
19. Fetterman, A. K., Bair, J. L., & Robinson, M. D. (2015). Submissive, inhibited, avoidant, and escape motivated: The correlates and consequences of arm-crossing. *Motivation Science, 1,* 37–46.
20. Wang, Y., & Griskevicius, V. (2014). Conspicuous consumption, relationships, and rivals: Women's luxury products as signals to other women. *Journal of Consumer Research, 40,* 834–854.
21. Levitt, A., & Leonard, K. E. (2015). Insecure attachment styles, relationship-drinking contexts, and marital alcohol problems: Testing the mediating role of relationship-specific drinking-to-cope motives. *Psychology of Addictive Behaviors, 29*(3), 696–705.
22. Rodriguez, L. M., Knee, C. R., & Neighbors, C. (2014). Relationships can drive some to drink: Relationship-contingent self-esteem and drinking problems. *Journal of Social and Personal Relationships, 31,* 270–290.

23. For information on how couples mimic each other's drinking: Lambe, L., Mackinnon, S. P., & Stewart, S. H. (2015). Dyadic conflict, drinking to cope, and alcohol-related problems: A psychometric study and longitudinal actor-partner interdependence model. *Journal of Family Psychology, 29,* 697–707.
24. Wiersma, J. D., & Fischer, J. L. (2014). Young adult drinking partnerships: Alcohol-related consequences and relationship problems six years later. *Journal of Studies on Alcohol and Drugs, 75,* 704–712.
25. Joel, S., Teper, R., & MacDonald, G. (2014). People overestimate their willingness to reject potential romantic partners by overlooking their concern for other people. *Psychological Science, 25,* 2233–2240.
26. For information on barriers to leaving relationships: Knopp, K. C., Rhoades, G. K., Stanley, S. M., & Markman, H. J. (2015). Stuck on you: How dedication moderates the way constraints feel. *Journal of Social and Personal Relationships, 32,* 119–137.
27. Gustavson, K., Nilsen, W., Orstavik, R., & Roysamb, E. (2014). Relationship quality, divorce, and well-being: Findings from a three-year longitudinal study. *Journal of Positive Psychology, 9,* 163–174.
28. For information on rebound relationships: Brumbaugh, C. C., & Fraley, R. C. (2015). Too fast too soon? An empirical investigation into rebound relationships. *Journal of Social and Personal Relationships, 32,* 99–118.
29. Young, S. L., Bippus, A. M., & Dunbar, N. E. (2015). Comparing romantic partners' perceptions of hurtful communication during conflict conversations. *Southern Communication Journal, 80,* 39–54.
30. Hofmann, W., Finkel, E. J., & Fitzsimons, G. M. (2015). Close relationships and self-regulation: How relationship satisfaction facilitates momentary goal pursuit. *Journal of Personality and Social Psychology, 109,* 434–452.
31. Koval, C. Z., vanDellen, M. R., Fitzsimons, G. M., & Ranby, K. W. (2015). The burden of responsibility: Interpersonal costs of high self-control. *Journal of Personality and Social Psychology, 108,* 750–766.
32. McDaniel, B. T., & Coyne, S. M. (2014). "Technoference": The interference of technology in couple relationships and implications for women's personal and relational well-being. *Psychology of Popular Media Culture* 5(1), 85–98. doi:10.1037/ppm0000065
33. Berrios, R., Totterdell, P., & Niven, K. (2015). Why do you make us feel good? Correlates and interpersonal consequences of affective presence in speed-dating. *European Journal of Personality, 29,* 72–82.
34. For a reference to the study, as well as background research on the impact of sharing positive news and being responsive when another person shares their good news: Otto, A. K., Laurenceau, J-P., Siegel,

S. D., & Belcher, A. J. (2015). Capitalizing on everyday positive events uniquely predicts daily intimacy and well-being in couples coping with breast cancer. *Journal of Family Psychology, 29*(1), 69–79.

35. Malouff, J. M., Mundy, S. A., Galea, T. R., & Bothma, V. N. (2015). Preliminary findings supporting a new model of how couples maintain excitement in romantic relationships. *The American Journal of Family Therapy, 43,* 227–237.
36. Graham, J. M., & Harf, M. R. (2015). Self-expansion and flow: The roles of challenge, skill, affect, and activation. *Personal Relationships, 22,* 45–64.
37. Girme, Y. U., Overall, N. C., & Faingataa, S. (2014). "Date nights" take two: The maintenance function of shared relationship activities. *Personal Relationships, 21,* 125–149.
38. For this whole section on how happy couples see the best in their partner: Murray, S. L. (1999). The quest for conviction: Motivated cognition in romantic relationships. *Psychological Inquiry, 10,* 23–34.
39. Murray, S. L., Holmes, J. G., & Griffin, D. W. (1996). The self-fulfilling nature of positive illusions in romantic relationships: Love is not blind, but prescient. *Journal of Personality and Social Psychology, 71,* 1155–1180.
40. Conley, T. D., Roesch, S. C., Peplau, L. A., & Gold, M. S. (2009). A test of positive illusions versus shared reality models of relationship satisfaction among gay, lesbian, and heterosexual couples. *Journal of Applied Social Psychology, 39,* 1417–1431.
41. Thai, S., & Lockwood, P. (2015). Comparing you = comparing me: Social comparisons of the expanded self. *Personality and Social Psychology Bulletin, 41,* 989–1004.
42. Morry, M. M., Kito, M., & Dunphy, L. (2014). How do I see you? Partner-enhancement in dating couples. *Canadian Journal of Behavioural Science, 46,* 356–365.
43. Luo, S., & Snider, A. G. (2009). Accuracy and biases in newlyweds' perceptions of each other. *Psychological Science, 20,* 1332–1339.
44. Day, L. C., Muise, A., Joel, S., & Impett, E. A. (2015). To do it or not to do it? How communally motivated people navigate sexual interdependence dilemmas. *Personality and Social Psychology Bulletin, 41,* 791–804.
45. McGraw, A. P., Warren, C., & Kan, C. (2015). Humorous complaining. *Journal of Consumer Research, 41,* 1153–1171.
46. For a similar variation on this writing activity: Morry, M. M., Kito, M., & Dunphy, L. (2014). How do I see you? Partner-enhancement in dating couples. *Canadian Journal of Behavioural Science, 46,* 356–365.

Chapter Five: Denial at the Level of Our Situation

1. For information on control and superstitions: Blanco, F., & Matute, H. (2015). Exploring the factors that encourage the illusions of control. *Experimental Psychology, 62,* 131–142; Li, S. (2015, February 13). Skipping the 13th floor. *The Atlantic.* Retrieved from www.theatlantic.com/technology/archive/2015/02/skipping-the-13th-floor/385448/; and Marmor, J. (1956). Some observations on superstition in contemporary life. *American Journal of Orthopsychiatry, 26,* 119–130.
2. Biner, P. M., Johnston, B. C., Summers, A. D., & Chudzynski, E. N. (2009). Illusory control as a function of the motivation to avoid randomly determined aversive outcomes. *Motivation and Emotion, 33,* 32–41.
3. Fenton-O'Creevy, M., Nicholson, N., Soane, E., & Willman, P. (2003). Trading on illusions: Unrealistic perceptions of control and trading performance. *Journal of Occupational and Organizational Psychology, 76,* 53–68.
4. Glavin, P., & Schieman, S. (2014). Control in the face of uncertainty: Is job insecurity a challenge to the mental health benefits of control beliefs? *Social Psychology Quarterly, 77,* 319–343.
5. For a review of the link between a sense of control and health: Turiano, N. A., Chapman, B. P., Agrigoroaei, S., Infurna, F. J., & Lachman, M. (2014). Perceived control reduces mortality risk at low, not high, education levels. *Health Psychology, 33,* 883–890.
6. Infurna, F. J., & Gerstorf, D. (2014). Perceived control relates to better functional health and lower cardio-metabolic risk: The mediating role of physical activity. *Health Psychology, 33,* 85–94.
7. Wagner, J., Hoppmann, C., Ram, N., & Gerstorf, D. (2015). Self-esteem is relatively stable late in life: The role of resources in the health, self-regulation, and social domains. *Developmental Psychology, 51,* 136–149.
8. Maddi, S. R. (2004). Hardiness: An operation of existential courage. *Journal of Humanistic Psychology, 44,* 279–298.
9. Langens, T. A. (2007). Regulatory focus and illusions of control. *Personality and Social Psychology Bulletin, 33,* 226–237.
10. Greenaway, K. H., Haslam, S. A., Cruwys, T., Branscombe, N. R., Ysseldyk, R., & Heldreth, C. (2015). From "we" to "me": Group identification enhances perceived personal control with consequences for health and well-being. *Journal of Personality and Social Psychology, 109,* 53–74.
11. For information on how people can make choices that go against their own interests, and how inattention can play a role in this: Suri, G., & Gross, J. J. (2015). The role of attention in motivated behavior. *Journal of Experimental Psychology: General, 144,* 864–872.
12. For holding off making choices, and how this is itself a choice: White, C. M., Hoffrage, U., & Reisen, N. (2015). Choice deferral can arise from absolute evaluations or relative comparisons. *Journal of Experimental Psychology: Applied, 21,* 140–157.

13. Gilbride, T. J., Inman, J. J., & Stilley, K. M. (2015). The role of within-trip dynamics in unplanned versus planned purchase behavior. *Journal of Marketing, 79,* 57–73.
14. Nagoshi, C. T. (1999). Perceived control of drinking and other predictors of alcohol use and problems in a college student sample. *Addiction Research, 7,* 291–306.
15. Khaylis, A., Trockel, M., & Taylor, C. B. (2009). Binge drinking in women at risk for developing eating disorders. *International Journal of Eating Disorders, 42,* 409–414.
16. Peter-Hagene, L. C., & Ullman, S. E. (2014). Social reactions to sexual assault disclosure and problem drinking: Mediating effects of perceived control and PTSD. *Journal of Interpersonal Violence, 29,* 1418–1437.
17. Lieberman, D. Z., Cioletti, A., Massey, S. H., Collantes, R. S., & Moore, B. B. (2014). Treatment preferences among problem drinkers in primary care. *International Journal of Psychiatry in Medicine, 47,* 231–240.
18. The National Intimate Partner and Sexual Violence Survey. (2015, March 10). Retrieved from www.cdc.gov/violenceprevention/nisvs/index.html
19. For information on the percentage of people who develop PTSD in the wake of intimate partner violence, and the relationship between the occurrence of abuse and the likelihood of developing PTSD: Lilly, M. M., Howell, K. H., & Graham-Bermann, S. (2015). World assumptions, religiosity, and PTSD in survivors of intimate partner violence. *Violence Against Women, 21,* 87–104.
20. For the ways people in abusive relationships rationalize the abuse: Whiting, J. B., Oka, M., & Fife, S. T. (2012). Appraisal distortions and intimate partner violence: Gender, power, and interaction. *Journal of Marital and Family Therapy, 38,* 133–149.
21. For information on the percentages of people who have been bullied at work, examples of workplace bullying, and how people cope: Dehue, F., Bolman, C., Vollink, T., & Pouwelse, M. (2012). Coping with bullying at work and health related problems. *International Journal of Stress Management, 19,* 175–197.
22. For information on reasons why people don't seek help to improve their physical mobility or safeguard against falling: Bunn, F., Dickinson, A., Barnett-Page, E., McInnes, E., & Horton, K. (2008). A systematic review of older people's perceptions of facilitators and barriers to participation in falls-prevention interventions. *Ageing & Society, 28,* 449–472.
23. Venetis, M. K., Robinson, J. D., & Kearney, T. (2015). Breast-cancer patients' participation behavior and coping during presurgical consultations: A pilot study. *Health Communication, 30,* 19–25.

24. Classen, S., Winter, S., & Lopez, E. D. S. (2009). Meta-synthesis of qualitative studies on older driver safety and mobility. *Occupation, Participation and Health, 29,* 24–31.
25. Coupe, C. (2014, December 4). 10 incredible acts of heroism by ordinary people. *Listverse.* Retrieved from http://listverse.com/2014/12/04/10-incredible-acts-of-heroism-by-ordinary-people/
26. For information on heroes and quick acting in the face of dire circumstances: Harvey, J., Erdos, G., & Turnbull, L. (2009). How do we perceive heroes? *Journal of Risk Research, 12,* 313–327.
27. For different forms of heroism: Franco, Z. E., Blau, K., & Zimbardo, P. G. (2011). Heroism: A conceptual analysis and differentiation between heroic action and altruism. *Review of General Psychology, 15,* 99–113.
28. Fagin-Jones, S., & Midlarsky, E. (2007). Courageous altruism: Personal and situational correlates of rescue during the Holocaust. *The Journal of Positive Psychology, 2,* 136–147.
29. For an excellent exploration of the beliefs people hold about themselves and their world, and how trauma can fly in the face of them: Janoff-Bulman, R. (1989). Assumptive worlds and the stress of traumatic events: Applications of the schema construct. *Social Cognition, 7,* 113–136.
30. Gigerenzer, G. (2006). Out of the frying pan into the fire: Behavioral reactions to terrorist attacks. *Risk Analysis, 26,* 347–351.
31. Haller, M. M., & Chassin, L. (2010). The reciprocal influences of perceived risk for alcoholism and alcohol use over time: Evidence for aversive transmission of parental alcoholism. *Journal of Studies on Alcohol and Drugs, 71,* 588–596.
32. Dillard, A. J., Midboe, A. M., & Klein, W. M. P. (2009). The dark side of optimism: Unrealistic optimism about problems with alcohol predicts subsequent negative event experiences. *Personality and Social Psychology Bulletin, 35,* 1540–1550.
33. Winter, J., & Wuppermann, A. (2014). Do they know what is at risk? Health risk perception among the obese. *Health Economics, 23,* 564–585.
34. Katapodi, M. C., Dodd, M. J., Lee, K. A., & Facione, N. C. (2009). Underestimation of breast cancer risk: Influence on screening behavior. *Oncology Nursing Forum, 36,* 306–314.
35. Thompson, S. C., Robbins, T., Payne, R., & Castillo, C. (2011). Message derogation and self-distancing denial: Situational and dispositional influences on the use of denial to protect against a threatening message. *Journal of Applied Social Psychology, 41,* 2816–2836.
36. Hevey, D., McGee, H. M., & Horgan, J. H. (2014). Comparative optimism among patients with coronary artery disease (CHD) is associated with fewer adverse clinical events 12 months later. *Journal of Behavioral Medicine, 37,* 300–307.

37. Wurm, S., & Benyamini, Y. (2014). Optimism buffers the detrimental effect of negative self-perceptions of ageing on physical and mental health. *Psychology and Health, 29*(7), 832–848.
38. For information on effects of procrastination: Mohsin, F. Z., & Ayub, N. (2014). The relationship between procrastination, delay of gratification, and job satisfaction among high school teachers. *Japanese Psychological Research, 56,* 224–234; and Rozental, A., Forsell, E., Svensson, A., Andersson, G., & Carlbring, P. (2015). Internet-based cognitive-behavioral therapy for procrastination: A randomized controlled trial. *Journal of Consulting and Clinical Psychology, 83,* 808–824.
39. For all of the information in this section on procrastination, time perspective, stress, and ways to address this: Sirois, H. M. (2014). Out of sight, out of time? A meta-analytic investigation of procrastination and time perspective. *European Journal of Personality, 28,* 511–520.
40. DeArmond, S., Matthews, R. A., & Bunk, J. (2014). Workload and procrastination: The roles of psychological detachment and fatigue. *International Journal of Stress Management, 21,* 137–161.
41. Levinson, A. H., Campo, S., Gascoigne, J., Jolly, O., Zakharyan, A., & Tran, Z. V. (2007). Smoking, but not smokers: Identity among college students who smoke cigarettes. *Nicotine and Tobacco Research, 9,* 845–852.
42. For information on denial of responsibility: Gosling, P., Denizeau, M., & Oberle, D. (2006). Denial of responsibility: A new mode of dissonance reduction. *Journal of Personality and Social Psychology, 90,* 722–733.
43. Sweeny, K., Shepperd, J. A., & Howell, J. L. (2012). Do as I say (not as I do): Inconsistency between behavior and values. *Basic and Applied Social Psychology, 34,* 128–135.
44. For a clear-cut description of Dr. Leon Festinger's Dissonance Theory: Gosling, P., Denizeau, M., & Oberle, D. (2006). Denial of responsibility: A new mode of dissonance reduction. *Journal of Personality and Social Psychology, 90,* 722–733.
45. Rubens, L., Gosling, P., Bonaiuto, M., Brisbois, X., & Moch, A. (2015). Being a hypocrite or committed while I am shopping? A comparison of the impact of two interventions on environmentally friendly behavior. *Environment and Behavior, 47,* 3–16.
46. Smith, A. J., Abeyta, A. A., Hughes, M., & Jones, R. T. (2015). Persistent grief in the aftermath of mass violence: The predictive roles of post-traumatic stress symptoms, self-efficacy, and disrupted worldview. *Psychological Trauma: Theory, Research, Practice, and Policy, 7,* 179–186.
47. Stavrova, O., & Ehlebracht, D. (2016). Cynical beliefs about human nature and income: Longitudinal and cross-cultural analyses. *Journal of Personality and Social Psychology 110*(1), 116–132. doi:10.1037/pspp0000050
48. MacKenzie, M. J., Vohs, K. D., & Baumeister, R. F. (2014). You didn't have to do that: Belief in free will promotes gratitude. *Personality and Social Psychology Bulletin, 40,* 1423–1434.

49. Webster, J. D., & Deng, X. C. (2015). Paths from trauma to interpersonal strength: Worldview, posttraumatic growth, and wisdom. *Journal of Loss and Trauma, 20,* 253–266.
50. Steele-Johnson, D., & Kalinoski, Z. T. (2014). Error framing effects on performance: Cognitive, motivational, and affective pathways. *The Journal of Psychology, 148,* 93–111.
51. Lin, C-C. (2015). Impact of gratitude on resource development and emotional well-being. *Social Behavior and Personality, 43,* 493–504.
52. Versey, H. S. (2015). Managing work and family: Do control strategies help? *Developmental Psychology, 51,* 1672–1681.
53. For a variation on this exercise: Peters, M. L., Flink, I. K., Boersma, K., & Linton, S. J. (2010). Manipulating optimism: Can imagining a best possible self be used to increase positive future expectancies? *The Journal of Positive Psychology, 5,* 204–211.

Chapter Six: Denial at the Level of Society

1. For the definition of conformity: Breckler, S. J., Olson, J. M., & Wiggins, E. C. (2006). *Social psychology alive.* Belmont, CA: Thomson/Wadsworth.
2. For information on the two reasons we conform: Raghunathan, R., & Corfman, K. (2006). Is happiness shared doubled and sadness shared halved? Social influence on enjoyment of hedonic experiences. *Journal of Marketing Research, 43,* 386–394.
3. For the point that people can guide us as we navigate situations: Breckler, S. J., Olson, J. M., & Wiggins, E. C. (2006). *Social psychology alive.* Belmont, CA: Thomson/Wadsworth.
4. Raghunathan, R., & Corfman, K. (2006). Is happiness shared doubled and sadness shared halved? Social influence on enjoyment of hedonic experiences. *Journal of Marketing Research, 43,* 386–394.
5. Ulloa, J. L., Marchetti, C., Taffou, M., & George, N. (2015). Only your eyes tell me what you like: Exploring the liking effect induced by other's gaze. *Cognition and Emotion, 29,* 460–470.
6. Parravano, A., Noguera, J. A., Hermida, P., & Tena-Sanchez, J. (2015). Field evidence of social influence in the expression of political preferences: The case of secessionists flags in Barcelona. *PLoS ONE, 10*(5). doi:10.1371/journal.pone.0125085
7. Hauge, K. E. (2015). Moral opinions are conditional on the behavior of others. *Review of Social Economy, 73,* 154–175.
8. Gilman, J. M., Treadway, M. T., Curran, M. T., Calderon, V., & Evins, A. E. (2015). Effect of social influence on effort-allocation for monetary rewards. *PLoS ONE, 10*(5). doi:10.1371/journal.pone.0126656
9. Li, N., Zhao, H. H., Walter, S. L., Zhang, X., & Yu, J. (2015). Achieving more with less: Extra milers' behavioral influences in teams. *Journal of Applied Psychology, 100,* 1025–1039.

10. Kormos, C., Gifford, R., & Brown, E. (2015). The influence of descriptive social norm information on sustainable transportation behavior: A field experiment. *Environment and Behavior, 47,* 479–501.
11. Litt, D. M., & Lewis, M. A. (2015). Examining the role of abstainer prototype favorability as a mediator of the abstainer-norms-drinking-behavior relationship. *Psychology of Addictive Behaviors, 29,* 467–472.
12. Liu, S., Wang, M., Bamberger, P., Shi, J., & Bacharach, S. B. (2015). The dark side of socialization: A longitudinal investigation of newcomer alcohol use. *Academy of Management Journal, 58,* 334–355.
13. Dallas, R., Field, M., Jones, A., Christiansen, P., Rose, A., & Robinson, E. (2014). Influenced but unaware: Social influence on alcohol drinking among social acquaintances. *Alcoholism: Clinical and Experimental Research, 38,* 1448–1453.
14. Kane, A. A., & Rink, F. (2015). How newcomers influence group utilization of their knowledge: Integrating versus differentiating strategies. *Group Dynamics: Theory, Research, and Practice, 19,* 91–105.
15. Coman, A., & Hirst, W. (2015). Social identity and socially shared retrieval-induced forgetting: The effects of group membership. *Journal of Experimental Psychology: General, 144,* 717–722.
16. Muir, K., Brown, C., & Madill, A. (2015). The fading affect bias: Effects of social disclosure to an interactive versus non-responsive listener. *Memory, 23,* 829–847.
17. Mumenthaler, C., & Sander, D. (2015). Autonomic integration of social information in emotion recognition. *Journal of Experimental Psychology: General, 144,* 392–399.
18. For information on the "foot-in-the-door" technique: Gueguen, N., & Pascual, A. (2015). Foot-in-the-door technique and problematic implicit request for help. *Swiss Journal of Psychology, 74,* 111–114.
19. Gueguen, N., Silone, F., David, M., & Pascual, A. (2015). The effect of the "evoking freedom" technique on an unusual and disturbing request. *Psychological Reports, 116,* 936–940.
20. For information on the influence of eyes on our behavior: Bodur, H. O., Duval, K. M., & Grohmann, B. (2015). Will you purchase environmentally friendly products? Using prediction requests to increase choice of sustainable products. *Journal of Business Ethics, 129,* 59–75.
21. For information on the benefits linked to social support, and the difference between online and "real-life" support: Trepte, S., Dienlin, T., & Reinecke, L. (2015). Influence of social support received in online and offline contexts on satisfaction with social support and satisfaction with life: A longitudinal study. *Media Psychology, 18,* 74–105.
22. Camozzato, A., Godinho, C., Varela, J., Kohler, C., Rinaldi, J., & Chaves, M. L. (2015). The complex role of having a confidant on the development of Alzheimer's disease in a community-based cohort of older people in Brazil. *Neuroepidemiology, 44,* 78–82.

23. Holt-Lunstad, J., Smith, T. B., Baker, M., Harris, T., & Stephenson, D. (2015). Loneliness and social isolation as risk factors for mortality: A meta-analytic review. *Perspectives on Psychological Science, 10,* 227–237.
24. For information on conformity: Lee, E. (2005). When placebic information differs from real information. *Communication Research, 32,* 615–645; and Sassenberg, K., Boos, M., & Rabung, S. (2005). Attitude change in face-to-face and computer-mediated communication: Private self-awareness as mediator and moderator. *European Journal of Social Psychology, 35,* 361–374.
25. For information on the soft sell: Breckler, S. J., Olson, J. M., & Wiggins, E. C. (2006). *Social psychology alive.* Belmont, CA: Thomson/Wadsworth.
26. For information on HIV-related denial and Holocaust denial: Chigwedere, P., & Essex, M. (2010). AIDS denialism and public health practice. *AIDS and Behavior, 14,* 237–247; and Lasson, K. (2007). Defending truth: Legal and psychological aspects of Holocaust denial. *Current Psychology, 26,* 223–266.
27. Fernandez, M., & Hauser, C. (2015, October 5). Texas mother teaches textbook company a lesson on accuracy. *New York Times.* Retrieved from www.nytimes.com/2015/10/06/us/publisher-promises-revisions-after-textbook-refers-to-african-slaves-as-workers.html?_r=0
28. For a thorough description of Dr. Cohen's types of denial, and of our tendency to turn away from suffering: Seu, I. B. (2010). "Doing denial": Audience reaction to human rights appeals. *Discourse and Society, 21,* 438–457.
29. For information on how the suffering of others can feel threatening, how we can cope by detaching, and how we are more likely to blame and refuse to help in this disconnected place: Cao, X., & Decker, D. (2015). Psychological distancing: The effects of narrative perspectives and levels of access to a victim's inner world on victim blame and helping intention. *International Journal of Nonprofit and Voluntary Sector Marketing, 20*(1), 12–14.
30. For information in this section on the mental adjustments people make when it comes to eating meat: Bastian, B., Loughnan, S., Haslam, N., & Radke, H. R. M. (2012). Don't mind meat? The denial of mind to animals used for human consumption. *Personality and Social Psychology Bulletin, 38,* 247–256.
31. For a description of how we minimize environmental problems to hold onto our notion of a fair universe: Feygina, I. (2013). Social justice and the human-environment relationship: Common systemic, ideological, and psychological roots and processes. *Social Justice Research, 26,* 363–381.

32. Campbell, T. H., & Kay, A. C. (2014). Solution aversion: On the relation between ideology and motivated disbelief. *Journal of Personality and Social Psychology, 107,* 809–824.
33. For information on ways of turning down the dial on environmental warnings: Opotow, S., & Weiss, L. (2000). Denial and the process of moral exclusion in environmental conflict. *Journal of Social Issues, 56,* 475–490.
34. For information on the four immeasurables: Rosenberg, E. L., Zanesco, A. P., King, B. G., Aichele, S. R., Jacobs, T. L., Bridwell, D.A., . . . Saron, C. (2015). Intensive meditation training influences emotional responses to suffering. *Emotion, 15,* 775–790.
35. For information on the experience of members of minority and majority groups when they interact: Tropp, L. R. (2003). The psychological impact of prejudice: Implications for intergroup contact. *Group Processes and Intergroup Relations, 6,* 131–149.
36. For information on how isms counteract equality, a value that a number of societies care about: Abrams, D., Houston, D. M., Van de Vyver, J., & Vasiljevic, M. (2015). Equality hypocrisy, inconsistency, and prejudice: The unequal application of the universal human right to equality. *Peace and Conflict: Journal of Peace Psychology, 21,* 28–46.
37. For information on biases: Raymond, J. (2013). Most of us are biased. *Nature, 495,* 33–34; and Staats, C. (2014). State of the science: Implicit bias review 2014. Retrieved from http://kirwaninstitute.osu.edu/wp-content/uploads/2014/03/2014-implicit-bias.pdf
38. Nelson, J. C., Adams, G., & Salter, P. S. (2013). The Marley hypothesis: Denial of racism reflects ignorance of history. *Psychological Science, 24,* 213–218.
39. For information on denial of racism: Apfelbaum, E. P., Sommers, S. R., & Norton, M. I. (2008). Seeing race and seeming racist? Evaluating strategic colorblindness in social interaction. *Journal of Personality and Social Psychology, 95,* 918–932; Knowles, E. D., Lowery, B. S., Chow, R. M., & Unzueta, M. M. (2014). Deny, distance, or dismantle? How White Americans manage a privileged identity. *Perspectives on Psychological Science, 9,* 594–609; and Neville, H. A., Awad, G. H., Brooks, J. E., Flores, M. P., & Bluemel, J. (2013). Color-blind racial ideology: Theory, training, and measurement implications in psychology. *American Psychologist, 68,* 455–466.
40. For information on the negative connections between not seeing racism and assorted social ills and injustices: Neville, H. A., & Awad, G. H. (2014). Why racial color-blindness is myopic. *American Psychologist, 69,* 313–314; and Neville, H. A., Awad, G. H., Brooks, J. E., Flores, M. P., & Bluemel, J. (2013). Color-blind racial ideology: Theory, training, and measurement implications in psychology. *American Psychologist, 68,* 455–466.

41. Cheng, H., Lin, S., & Cha, C. H. (2015). Perceived discrimination, intergenerational family conflicts, and depressive symptoms in foreign-born and U.S.-born Asian American emerging adults. *Asian American Journal of Psychology, 6,* 107–116.
42. Lee, Y., Muennig, P., Kawachi, I., & Hatzenbuehler, M. L. (2015). Effects of racial prejudice on the health of communities: A multilevel survival analysis. *American Journal of Public Health, 105,* 2349–2355.
43. For information on how racism undermines fairness and justice in society: Gill, R. D., Lazos, S. R., & Waters, M. M. (2011). Are judicial performance evaluations fair to women and minorities? A cautionary tale from Clark County, Nevada. *Law and Society Review, 45,* 731–759; Glaser, J., Martin, K. D., & Kahn, K. B. (2015). Possibility of death sentence has divergent effect on verdicts for Black and White defendants. *Law and Human Behavior, 39,* 539–546; and Howell, T. M., Harrison, D. A., Burris, E. R., & Detert, J. R. (2015). Who gets credit for input? Demographic and structural status cues in voice recognition. *Journal of Applied Psychology, 100,* 1765–1784.
44. For the definitions of hostile sexism and benevolent sexism: Glick, P., & Fiske, S. T. (2001). An ambivalent alliance: Hostile and benevolent sexism as complementary justifications for gender inequality. *American Psychologist, 56,* 109–118.
45. For information on how men and women both gravitate toward benevolent sexism: Connelly, K., & Heesacker, M. (2012). Why is benevolent sexism appealing? Associations with system justification and life satisfaction. *Psychology of Women Quarterly, 36,* 432–443.
46. Becker, J. C., & Wright, S. C. (2011). Yet another dark side of chivalry: Benevolent sexism undermines and hostile sexism motivates collective action for social change. *Journal of Personality and Social Psychology, 101,* 62–77.
47. For information on how sexism undermines women in the workforce: Basford, T. E., Offermann, L. R., & Behrend, T. S. (2014). Do you see what I see? Perceptions of gender microaggressions in the workplace. *Psychology of Women Quarterly, 38,* 340–349; Rudman, L. A., & Kilianski, S. E. (2000). Implicit and explicit attitudes toward female authority. *Personality and Social Psychology Bulletin, 26,* 1315–1328; Sayers, R. C. (2012). The cost of being female: Critical comment on Block. *Journal of Business Ethics, 106,* 519–524; and Fact sheet: New steps to advance equal pay on the seventh anniversary of the Lilly Ledbetter fair pay act. (2016, January 29). Retrieved from www.whitehouse.gov/the-press-office/2016/01/29/fact-sheet-new-steps-advance-equal-pay-seventh-anniversary-lilly
48. Desai, S. D., Chugh, D., & Brief, A. P. (2014). The implications of marriage structure for men's workplace attitudes, beliefs, and behaviors toward women. *Administrative Science Quarterly, 59,* 330–365.

49. Hammond, M. D., & Overall, N. C. (2014). Endorsing benevolent sexism magnifies willingness to dissolve relationships when facing partner-ideal discrepancies. *Personal Relationships, 21,* 272–287.
50. Kutner, J. (2015, April 9). A majority of Americans support gender equality—so why don't they identify as feminists? *Salon.* Retrieved from www.salon.com/2015/04/09/a_majority_of_americans_support_gender_equality_so_why_dont_they_identify_as_feminists/
51. Voigt, K. (2014, September 16). Who pays? NerdWallet study finds gender roles remain strong among couples. NerdWallet. Retrieved from www.nerdwallet.com/blog/finance/who-pays-first-date-gender-roles-couples/
52. For information on the continued, open approval of heterosexism: Callender, K. A. (2015). Understanding antigay bias from a cognitive-affective-behavioral perspective. *Journal of Homosexuality, 62,* 782–803.
53. For information on heterosexism and workplace discrimination: Graham, H. E., Frame, M. C., & Kenworthy, J. B. (2014). The moderating effect of prior attitudes on intergroup face-to-face contact. *Journal of Applied Social Psychology, 44,* 547–556.
54. Herek, G. M. (2009). Hate crimes and stigma-related experiences among sexual minority adults in the United States: Prevalence estimates from a national probability sample. *Journal of Interpersonal Violence, 24,* 54–74.
55. For information on the link between gender norms, heterosexist-motivated aggression, and alcohol: Leone, R. M., & Parrott, D. J. (2015). Dormant masculinity: Moderating effects of acute alcohol intoxication on the relation between male role norms and antigay aggression. *Psychology of Men & Masculinity, 16,* 183–194; and Parrott, D. J., & Lisco, C. G. (2015). Effects of alcohol and sexual prejudice on aggression toward sexual minorities. *Psychology of Violence, 5,* 256–265.
56. For information on the harmful impact of anti-weight bias: Ratcliffe, D., & Ellison, N. (2015). Obesity and internalized weight stigma: A formulation model for an emerging psychological problem. *Behavioural and Cognitive Psychotherapy, 43,* 239–252.
57. Brochu, P. M., Pearl, R. L., Puhl, R. M., & Brownell, K. D. (2014). Do media portrayals of obesity influence support for weight-related medical policy? *Health Psychology, 33,* 197–200.
58. For a description of the impact of negative stereotypes on older adults and stereotype threat: Lamont, R. A., Swift, H. J., & Abrams, D. (2015). A review and meta-analysis of age-based stereotype threat: Negative stereotypes, not facts, do the damage. *Psychology and Aging, 30,* 180–193.
59. For information on aging stereotypes, worries about aging, and memory concerns: Pearman, A., Hertzog, C., & Gerstorf, D. (2014). Little evidence for links between memory complaints and memory performance

in very old age: Longitudinal analyses from the brain aging study. *Psychology and Aging, 29,* 828–842.

60. For information on how contact reduces ageism: Hutchison, P., Fox, E., Laas, A. M., Matharu, J., & Urzi, S. (2010). Anxiety, outcome expectancies, and young people's willingness to engage in contact with the elderly. *Educational Gerontology, 36,* 1008–1021.
61. For information on how contact reduces racism: Lemmer, G., & Wagner, U. (2015). Can we really reduce ethnic prejudice outside the lab? A meta-analysis of direct and indirect contact interventions. *European Journal of Social Psychology, 45,* 152–168; and Seger, C. R., Smith, E. R., Percy, E. J., & Conrey, F. R. (2014). Reach out and reduce prejudice: The impact of interpersonal touch on intergroup liking. *Basic and Applied Social Psychology, 36,* 51–58.
62. For information on how contact reduces heterosexism: Bartos, S. E., Berger, I., & Hegarty, P. (2014). Interventions to reduce sexual prejudice: A study-space analysis and meta-analytic review. *Journal of Sex Research, 51,* 363–382; and Graham, H. E., Frame, M. C., & Kenworthy, J. B. (2014). The moderating effect of prior attitudes on intergroup face-to-face contact. *Journal of Applied Social Psychology, 44,* 547–556.
63. For information on how contact reduces body weight prejudice: Koball, A. M., & Carels, R. A. (2015). Intergroup contact and weight bias reduction. *Translational Issues in Psychological Science, 1,* 298–306.
64. For information on how imagining contact can lessen prejudice: Turner, R. N., & Crisp, R. J. (2010). Imagining intergroup contact reduces implicit prejudice. *British Journal of Social Psychology, 49,* 129–142.
65. For information on how media portrayals that challenge stereotypes can reduce prejudice: Ramasubramanian, S. (2015). Using celebrity news stories to effectively reduce racial/ethnic prejudice. *Journal of Social Issues, 71,* 123–138.
66. For information on the effect of media on transgender prejudice: Sneed, T. (2014, June 6). What transgender looks like in pop culture. *U.S. News and World Report.* Retrieved from www.usnews.com/news/articles/2014/06/06/laverne-cox-and-the-state-of-trans-representation-in-pop-culture; and Tompkins, T. L., Shields, C. N., Hillman, K. M., & White, K. (2015). Reducing stigma toward the transgender community: An evaluation of a humanizing and perspective-taking intervention. *Psychology of Sexual Orientation and Gender Diversity, 2,* 34–42.
67. For information on education and reducing sexism: Becker, J. C., Zawadzki, M. J., & Shields, S. A. (2014). Confronting and reducing sexism: A call for research on intervention. *Journal of Social Issues, 70,* 603–614; and Becker, J. C., & Swim, J. K. (2012). Reducing endorsement of benevolent and modern sexist beliefs. *Social Psychology, 43,* 127–137.
68. Fehr, J., & Sassenberg, K. (2010). Willing and able: How internal motivation and failure help to overcome prejudice. *Group Processes and Intergroup Relations, 13,* 167–181.

Chapter Seven: Denial at the Level of Life and Death

1. For information about aging biases across nations and cultures: North, M. S., & Fiske, S. T. (2015). Modern attitudes toward older adults in the aging world: A cross-cultural meta-analysis. *Psychological Bulletin, 141,* 993–1021.
2. For information on the stereotype that older people are less happy than younger people: Lacey, H. P., Kierstead, T. A., & Morey, D. (2012). De-biasing the age-happiness judgments across the lifespan. *Journal of Happiness Studies, 13,* 647–658.
3. For information on negative assumptions about aging and unhappiness, and how the research contradicts this: Lacey, H. P., Smith, D. S., & Ubel, P. A. (2006). Hope I die before I get old: Mispredicting happiness across the adult lifespan. *Journal of Happiness Studies, 7,* 167–182.
4. Carstensen, L. L., Pasupathi, M., Mayr, U., & Nesselroade, J. R. (2000). Emotional experiences in everyday life across the adult life span. *Journal of Personality and Social Psychology, 79,* 644–655.
5. For information on the relationship between health and happiness, and for the results of this study: Angner, E., Ghandhi, J., Purvis, K. W., Amante, D., & Allison, J. (2013). Daily functioning, health status, and happiness in older adults. *Journal of Happiness Studies, 14,* 1563–1574.
6. Mock, S. E., & Eibach, R. P. (2011). Aging attitudes moderate the effect of subjective age on psychological well-being: Evidence from a 10-year longitudinal study. *Personality and Aging, 26,* 979–986.
7. For information on aging stereotypes and attitudes: Lund, A., & Engelsrud, G. (2008). "I am not that old": Interpersonal experiences of thriving and threats at a senior centre. *Ageing & Society, 28,* 675–692; and Weiss, D., & Lang, F. R. (2012). "They" are old but "I" feel younger: Age-group dissociation as a self-protective strategy in old age. *Psychology and Aging, 27,* 153–163.
8. Levy, B. R., Slade, M. D., & Gill, T. M. (2006). Hearing decline predicted by elders' stereotypes. *Journal of Gerontology, 61*(2), P82–P87.
9. Levy, B. R., & Leifheit-Limson, E. (2009). The stereotype-matching effect: Greater influence on functioning when age stereotypes correspond to outcomes. *Psychology and Aging, 24,* 230–233.
10. Levy, B. R., Pilver, C., Chung, P. H., & Slade, M. D. (2014). Subliminal strengthening: Improving older individuals' physical function over time with an implicit-age-stereotype intervention. *Psychological Science, 25,* 2127–2135.
11. For this entire section on how associating unwanted bodily changes with age can be a barrier to exercise, and why this might be the case: O'Connor, B. P., Rousseau, F., & Maki, S. A. (2004). Physical exercise and experienced bodily changes: The emergence of benefits and limits on benefits. *International Journal of Aging and Human Development, 59,* 177–203.

12. Wolff, J. K., Warner, L. M., Ziegelmann, J. P., & Wurm, S. (2014). What do targeting positive views on ageing add to a physical activity intervention in older adults? Results from a randomized controlled trial. *Psychology and Health, 29,* 915–932.
13. Williams, P. T. (2015). Lower risk of Alzheimer's disease mortality with exercise, statin, and fruit intake. *Journal of Alzheimer's Disease, 44,* 1121–1129.
14. For an excellent summary of Terror Management Theory and the scientific evidence for it: Maxfield, M., John, S., & Pyszczynski, T. (2014). A terror management perspective on the role of death-related anxiety in psychological dysfunction. *The Humanistic Psychologist, 42,* 35–53. Please note that this reference informed the description of how we turn down the dial when thoughts of death are at the forefront and at the back of our minds.
15. Bassett, J. F., & Dabbs, J. M., Jr. (2003). Evaluating explicit and implicit death attitudes in funeral and university students. *Mortality, 8,* 352–371.
16. Smith, L. M., & Kasser, T. (2014). Mortality salience increases defensive distancing from people with terminal cancer. *Death Studies, 38,* 44–53.
17. Yaakobi, E. (2015). Desire to work as a death anxiety buffer mechanism. *Experimental Psychology, 62,* 110–122.
18. Hohman, Z. P., & Hogg, M. A. (2015). Mortality salience, self-esteem, and defense of the group: Mediating role of in-group identification. *Journal of Applied Social Psychology, 45,* 80–89.
19. Kneer, J., & Rieger, D. (2015). The memory remains: How heavy metal fans buffer against the fear of death. *Psychology of Popular Media Culture.* doi:10.1037/ppm0000072
20. For information on how the majority of cultures value the concept of an afterlife in some form: Maxfield, M., John, S., & Pyszczynski, T. (2014). A terror management perspective on the role of death-related anxiety in psychological dysfunction. *The Humanistic Psychologist, 42,* 35–53.
21. Wisman, A., & Goldenberg, J. L. (2005). From the grave to the cradle: Evidence that mortality salience engenders a desire for offspring. *Journal of Personality and Social Psychology, 89,* 46–61.
22. McCabe, S., Arndt, J., Goldenberg, J. L., Vess, M., Vail, K. E., III., Gibbons, F. X., & Rogers, R. (2015). The effect of visualizing healthy eaters and mortality reminders on nutritious grocery purchases: An integrative terror management and prototype willingness analysis. *Health Psychology, 34,* 279–282.
23. For information on how our health intentions change depending on whether we're focusing on death or not, as well as the possible explanation described here for why this change may occur: Bevan, A. L., Maxfield, M., & Bultmann, M. N. (2014). The effects of age and

death awareness on intentions for healthy behaviours. *Psychology and Health, 29,* 405–421.

24. Goldenberg, J. L., Pyszczynski, T., Greenberg, J., Solomon, S., Kluck, B., & Cornwell, R. (2001). I am not an animal: Mortality salience, disgust, and the denial of human creatureliness. *Journal of Experimental Psychology: General, 103,* 427–435.
25. For information on how we become more motivated to separate ourselves from elements of our body, including the notion of sex, in response to thoughts of our own death: Goldenberg, J. L., Cox, C. R., Pyszczynski, T., Greenberg, J., & Solomon, S. (2002). Understanding human ambivalence about sex: The effects of stripping sex of meaning. *Journal of Sex Research, 39,* 310–320; and Goldenberg, J. L. (2005). The body stripped down: An existential account of the threat posed by the physical body. *Current Directions in Psychological Science, 14,* 224–228.
26. Routledge, C., Ostafin, B., Juhl, J., Sedikides, C., Cathey, C., & Liao, J. (2010). Adjusting to death: The effects of mortality salience and self-esteem on psychological well-being, growth motivation, and maladaptive behavior. *Journal of Personality and Social Psychology, 99,* 897–916.
27. For information on the impact of thoughts of death when people are unhappy in life and reflect on failure: Hayes, J., Ward, C. L., & McGregor, I. (2015). Why bother? Death, failure, and fatalistic withdrawal from life. *Journal of Personality and Social Psychology.* doi:10.1037/pspp0000039
28. For perspectives on the life-giving value of acknowledging our death: Wong, P. T. P., & Tomer, A. (2011). Beyond terror and denial: The positive psychology of death acceptance. *Death Studies, 35,* 99–106.
29. King, L. A., Hicks, J. A., & Abdelkhalik, J. (2009). Death, life, scarcity, and value: An alternative perspective on the meaning of death. *Psychological Science, 20,* 1459–1462.
30. Jiang, D., Fung, H. H., Sims, T., Tsai, J. L., & Zhang, F. (2015). Limited time perspective increases the value of calm. *Emotion 16*(1), 52–56. doi:10.1037/emo0000094
31. Frias, A., Watkins, P. C., Webber, A. C., & Froh, J. J. (2011). Death and gratitude: Death reflection enhances gratitude. *The Journal of Positive Psychology, 6,* 154–162.
32. For the activity that part of this first exercise was adapted from: Masters, J. L., & Holley, L. M. (2006). A glimpse of life at 67: The modified future-self worksheet. *Educational Gerontology, 32,* 261–269.
33. To find the full poem that this piece came from: Dickinson, E. (n.d.). Because I could not stop for death. Retrieved April 9, 2016, from www.poets.org/poetsorg/poem/because-i-could-not-stop-death-479

ABOUT THE AUTHOR

Dr. Holly Parker, or Dr. Holly, as she's more playfully known, is a psychologist with a passion for empowering individuals to cultivate the sort of life that reflects what they sincerely wish for, one that is authentic, gratifying, and joyful for them.

She obtained her PhD in experimental psychopathology from Harvard University, where she conducted research and was a Karen Stone Fellow and Sackler Scholar. Filled with an inner fire to help uplift people's lives through human connection, Dr. Parker re-specialized in clinical psychology at the University of Massachusetts, Amherst.

Presently, she zestfully engages in clinical work, teaching, public education, and writing. She is a lecturer at Harvard University, where she teaches the popular course "The Psychology of Close Relationships." She is also a practicing psychologist and an associate director of training at the Edith Nourse Rogers Memorial Veterans Hospital. In her clinical practice, people have given Dr. Parker the honor of joining them as they draw nearer to those formidable yet ultimately freeing spaces in life that they would, understandably, much rather bypass.

She is also the author of the forthcoming *If We're Together, Why Do I Feel So Alone?* (Berkley Books, 2017), which walks alongside readers hoping to mend emotional unavailability in their romantic relationships. Additionally, Dr. Parker is an author and co-author of several scientific papers in peer-reviewed journals, as well as a chapter on suicide bereavement in *The Oxford Handbook of Suicide and Self-Injury* (Oxford University Press, 2014).

Dr. Parker also delves into an assortment of topics on the dappled road of life in her blog (www.drhollyparker.com) and in press interviews through outlets such as *SELF Magazine, Prevention, Chicago Tribune, Psychology Today, ABC News,* and *The Saturday Evening Post.*

She lives in Boston with Guille, her extremely cool husband and kindred spirit, relishes running, studying Spanish, time travel stories, and *The Walking Dead,* and has no skill whatsoever in pet training.

ABOUT HAZELDEN PUBLISHING

As part of the Hazelden Betty Ford Foundation, Hazelden Publishing offers both cutting-edge educational resources and inspirational books. Our print and digital works help guide individuals in treatment and recovery, and their loved ones. Professionals who work to prevent and treat addiction also turn to Hazelden Publishing for evidence-based curricula, digital content solutions, and videos for use in schools, treatment programs, correctional programs, and electronic health records systems. We also offer training for implementation of our curricula.

Through published and digital works, Hazelden Publishing extends the reach of healing and hope to individuals, families, and communities affected by addiction and related issues.

For more information about Hazelden publications,
please call **800-328-9000**
or visit us online at **hazelden.org/bookstore**.

OTHER TITLES THAT MAY INTEREST YOU

The Next Happy
Let Go of the Life You Planned and Find a New Way Forward

Tracey Cleantis

When the best option is to let go of the life you planned for yourself and find a new path, a world of possibilities can surprisingly open up. Learn whether it is time to let go, and if so, how to move through your grief and find your way forward in *The Next Happy.*

Order No. 7768, also available as an e-book

Choosing a Good Life
Lessons from People Who Have Found Their Place in the World

Ali Berman

Discover the common approaches and qualities of those who, despite life's adversities, are at peace in the world—and learn how you can be too.

Order No. 7538, also available as an e-book

What Went Right
Reframe Your Thinking for a Happier Now

Eileen Bailey and Michael G. Wetter, PsyD

Through practical, easy-to-understand principles and techniques, as well as real-life examples, *What Went Right* teaches you to recognize and intervene on self-defeating thought processes.

Order No. 9610, also available as an e-book

For more information or to order these or other resources from Hazelden Publishing, call **800-328-9000** or visit **hazelden.org/bookstore**.